GRE

Se

Life

OF BRITAIN AND EUROPE

GREEN GUIDE

Seashore Life

OF BRITAIN AND EUROPE

bob gibbons

ILLUSTRATED BY denys ovenden
melanie perkins • helen senior

SELECT EDITIONS

This edition published in 2003 by
Selectabook Ltd.
Roundway, Devizes
Wiltshire SN10 2HT

First published in 1991 by New Holland Publishers (UK) Ltd

1 3 5 7 9 10 8 6 4 2

ISBN 1 84330 510 0

Phototypeset by AKM Associates (UK) Ltd
Reproduction by Scantrans Pte Ltd
Printed and bound in Singapore by
Kyodo Printing Co (Singapore) Pte Ltd

The publishers acknowledge with thanks the assistance of Andrea Bassil and the Bournemouth & Poole College of Art and Design

Contents

Introduction

This book is a simple colour guide to 150 of the plants and animals most likely to be seen in the intertidal areas around the coasts of Europe; it can be taken in a pocket on to the shore, where the animals themselves can be compared directly with the paintings. Many more than 150 species occur in this narrow band where land meets sea and we have therefore had to be highly selective. First, we have excluded mobile species that move in from other habitats, such as sea birds, or terrestrial birds like herons, that regularly feed on the seashore, or mammals like the otter; second, we have excluded rarities, unless they are exceptionally conspicuous or interesting; and third, we have generally excluded species that are difficult to identify, or we have featured one species as a representative of a large similar group. The selection includes a good range of the species that people are likely to find and be able to identify.

There are two ways in which the book can be used to identify any new species. First, as it is relatively small, a search can be made through all the illustrations for something similar, and then the text can be checked to confirm details such as the distribution, or structural details not visible. Alternatively, the classification guide at the end of this introductory section can be used to try to narrow down the possibilities to one main group, which can then be checked in the main illustrated section. The species are laid out in taxonomic order – i.e. with all related species together – rather than by habitats, colour, or any other criteria. If a species resembles an illustration, but is not quite like it, check the text for information on variability that is not illustrated, or for similar species.

In either event, always remember to take the book with you to the shore. If you take organisms away to identify, it may not only be harmful to the individuals concerned (and anything living on them), but you may also find that you do not have all the information that you require. With a seaweed, for example, you may need the shape of the holdfast, or you may need to search around for an example with fruiting bodies – these will be missed if just one frond is brought home to look at.

Looking at Seashore Life

The seashore is quite unlike any terrestrial habitat, and the plants and animals that occur there are generally very different in form from their land-based relatives. Many of the straightforward structural and behavioural differences that allow us to distinguish plants from animals break down on the seashore; plants are no longer just green, but all sorts of colours; there are animals that look like plants, and vice versa, and complex colonies of creatures of which the basic units are quite obscure to the casual observer. It is for this reason that the normal restriction of field guides to one biological group – e.g. birds, insects, or flowers – is not followed here, and the whole habitat is covered instead.

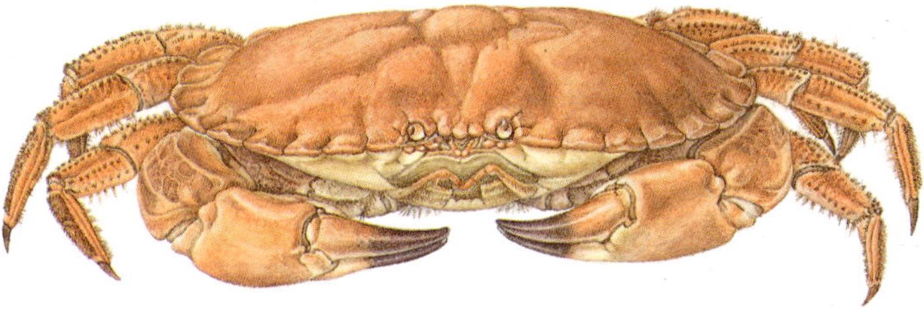

The way in which one has to look at the seashore is necessarily different from the way in which we study terrestrial habitats, too, though there are similarities with the study of pond life. The intertidal area allows us a fleeting glimpse of some of the creatures that live under the surface of the sea for some or all of their lives, which only become exposed as the tide goes out, twice a day. The organisms that live in the most accessible parts, near the high-tide mark, are, naturally, those that can stand most exposure to air, sunlight and fresh water in the form of rain – this area is usually the least varied and interesting part of the shore. As you go further down the beach the organisms that grow or live there are exposed for successively shorter times, until you eventually reach low-water mark. This is the richest area of study, but of course it can be reached by normal means only for very short periods. This is further complicated by the fact that the amplitude of tides varies according to the cycles of the moon, and the time of year, and therefore the very lowest parts of the shore are exposed only once a month, or just twice a year for the extreme low-tide zone; these areas contain the most species of all the intertidal areas, but it needs planning and a knowledge of the tidal cycle to get to see them.

Introduction

It is perfectly possible to see a range of intertidal animals, and washed-up marine creatures, without any special equipment or knowledge, just by following the tide out and looking in likely areas. However, you can see a much wider range of creatures, and more species, with a little planning and some simple equipment.

First, consult some tide-tables to find out when low tides are in your location. If you can possibly get information on the height of high tides, by deduction you can also discover the dates of the lowest tides, since the highest tides are accompanied by the lowest tides. If you are in an area only briefly, try to select the day which has the lowest tide, assuming that such lows occur at a reasonable time of day. If you can choose freely when you visit the seashore, it is well worth finding out when the very lowest tides will occur, and visiting then – the best are generally around the September equinox, when extreme low tides are combined with an excellent range of organisms to be seen.

A few items of equipment make it much easier to find and see organisms. Some white plastic margarine or ice-cream containers (between 1 and 4 litres capacity) are easily stacked and carried, and ideal for examining material in. Anything emerging from, for example, some seaweed, can quickly be seen and examined, whilst larger creatures can be kept temporarily while you identify them. A strong, long-handled net is extremely useful – the mesh size will affect what you catch, though you will find that fine meshes can be a nuisance as they trap everything and are therefore slow to use and easily broken. A very small hand net is invaluable, to allow removal of items from containers, or for catching animals in small pools. Clear plastic containers are useful for examining animals from all angles, and a hand lens (about ×10 magnification) will reveal many beautiful and unsuspected details on static subjects. If you plan to take photographs protect your camera from salt water and spray by carrying it in a waterproof container, only removing it briefly for the actual exposure – salt water ruins cameras very quickly. Finally, a notebook, pencil and one or more field guides are essential.

Safety on the Seashore

Looking at seashore life is safe enough if you take some reasonable precautions. The tide can advance extremely rapidly, especially over gently shelving beaches, so it is important to know the time of low tide and to check your return route. An innocent-seeming depression can quickly become an impassable barrier in areas where there is a marked tidal range. If you are working somewhere exposed, you also need to beware of sudden larger waves that may overbalance you on slippery rocks. It is best to wear plastic sandals or other suitable footwear, which not only increase your speed of movement but also protect against broken glass, sharp stones and stinging organisms like weever fish.

Zonation

Because of the regular way in which tides move in and out, exposing different parts of the shore for different times, there is a clear zoning of seashore life according to how tolerant different species are of exposure to air and sunlight. The zoning is not always clearly visible, especially on sandy shores and irregular shores with variable changes in level. At other times, it can be extremely well marked, with clearly visible bands of differently coloured plants extending down the shore – this is most easily seen on evenly sloped rocky shores. Because many species are quite precise in their requirements, a knowledge of this zonation can aid in identification if you take account of where the organism was found growing. It does not, of course, apply to washed-up or dislodged specimens, which can occur at any level.

The highest zone is the *splash zone*. Although this is above the levels of the highest tides, it is strongly affected by salt spray, especially on exposed coasts, and the resident life is directly influenced by this. Black and orange-coloured lichens are particularly characteristic of this zone, together with salt-tolerant flowering plants such as thrift, but no seaweeds normally occur here.

The highest zone that is regularly inundated is the *upper shore*, though it is usually defined as the area above mean high water, but below the line reached by the highest spring tides – i.e. it is not inundated by every high tide. This zone has relatively limited seashore life, but it includes channelled wrack, a few molluscs, some lichens, and much strand-line debris. Although poor in species, what there is may occur in large quantities.

The extensive area of shore between the average high-water level and the average low-water level is known as the *middle shore*. This area is covered and uncovered by every tide, and it makes up the bulk of what is thought of as the shore. Most of the typical seashore plants and animals occur here, often in great abundance, and there is a certain amount of zoning within this section, though it is not always visible.

Below the average low-water level, there is a further area of shore that is accessible only at spring tide lows – i.e. on lower-than-average tides. This is known as the *lower shore*. It is not accessible

every day, but it does support a fascinating range of creatures, including many delicate species that are unable to withstand much exposure. It is the closest we can get to seeing true marine life without diving.

Seashore Habitats

Seashores vary enormously in character, from exposed rocky coasts to sheltered estuaries or salt marshes. Each type of coast supports a different range of organisms, though of course the divisions between habitat types are not always clear cut, and in any case a number of mobile or adaptable species may occur in more than one shore type. The main shore types that can be recognised are: rocky shores, sandy shores, shingle and muddy shores, with rock pools as a distinctive subdivision. These relate to the underlying geology of the coast, to the degree of exposure to wave action, and to the offshore currents and sediments.

The Rocky Shore

Rocky shores can be divided into exposed and sheltered areas, though of course there is overlap between the two. The sheltered rocky shore is probably the most rewarding of all seashore habitats for looking at nature, with very large numbers of species occurring, often in great abundance. In general, rocky shores of either type are most frequent down the western seaboards of Europe, especially in Britain and Ireland, France, Spain and Portugal. Relatively small changes in alignment can mean the difference between being sheltered or exposed, and the two types can occur frequently in close juxtaposition, often with sandy beaches in between, offering immense opportunities for finding species.

The rock type has an important bearing on the fauna and flora to be found. To some extent, attached species are directly influenced by the chemical nature of the rock substrate, but more significant is the hardness of the rock and the way in which it weathers. A very fast-eroding rock supports relatively few species since they are constantly being sloughed off, though a moderately soft rock may be very rich, allowing easy attachment and weathering into a wide variety of niches for creatures to fill. The amount of pools, cracks and indentations in the rock has an important bearing on the amount of life supported, though it may not always be easier to see or catch.

Introduction

Rock pools are a feature of rocky shores and they have a particular life of their own. Conditions within them are unlike the open shore, since the life within them remains submerged whatever the state of the tide, but they are subject to increased light, warming up, dilution of the salinity by rain water and changes in the oxygen/carbon dioxide balance. As might be expected, the higher up the shore a rock pool is, the more it is subject to these changes, and – generally speaking – the less diverse the life it supports. The best rock pools of all are well down the shore, not too exposed, deep enough and large enough to minimise fluctuations in temperature on very hot or very cold days, and preferably with additional dark crannies or overhanging areas. Such places will probably be full of life, though it is not necessarily readily visible. Smaller pools are usually much easier to study, to start with. The best pool-forming rock types are granite, some shales, hard limestones, such as Carboniferous limestone, and basalt.

Shingle Beaches

By contrast with rocky shores, shingle beaches are probably the least diverse of intertidal environments. Shingle is made up of vast numbers of loose rounded stones, from pea-sized to boulder-sized, which are characteristically very mobile and unstable. On some parts of the coast, there are enormous stretches of shingle, such as the 30km Chesil beach in Dorset. In rough weather, shingle moves around considerably and smaller pebbles can easily be seen, and heard, to move. It is this intense degree of mobility that prevents most forms of life from getting a foothold, or which soon grinds them off again if they do. The middle and lower shore of a shingle beach is virtually devoid of life. Higher up, mobile invertebrates may scavenge in large numbers amongst detritus along the drift line. Above high-water mark, a few flowering plants such as Sea Pea, *Lathyrus japonicus*, and Yellow Horned Poppy, *Glaucium flavum*, can survive in this harsh environment, and a number of birds choose undisturbed shingle to nest on.

Sandy Shores

Sandy beaches are the most familiar type of shore and the one around which vast holiday industries have developed throughout the world. However, they are nothing like as rich in species as a sheltered rocky shore.

Sand is made up of masses of tiny grains, of varying size, shape and character, though always small enough to pack together tightly.

They are mobile, as with shingle, though often appear less so since they are quieter and usually occur in flatter situations. They are also subject to severe wind movement when exposed for long.

The exposed surface of sand supports very little life. However, there is rather more life below the surface, some of which emerges to feed when the tide covers it. Oxygen and water are trapped in the tiny spaces between grains, allowing resident species to maintain a reasonably stable environment below the surface. Typical sandy beach residents include lugworms, various molluscs such as cockles and tellins, shrimps, and some fishes. In some parts of the world, large populations of crabs burrow in the sand.

Muddy Shores and Salt Marshes

In very sheltered situations where the force of the sea is minimal, such as estuaries and bays, then the very smallest suspended particles in the sea are deposited as mud or silt. The mudflats of such places as Poole Harbour and Chichester Harbour, or long stretches of the north Norfolk coast, are familiar to many people.

The sheltered nature of muddy situations allows many species to do well, especially as such places may be very high in nutrients. Although the range of species is not usually large, the number and density of animals is often huge. Mudflats are one of the favoured feeding areas of vast numbers of waders and wildfowl in winter, as they are full of food and frost-free. Where the force of wave action falls below a certain threshold, and the land is not submerged totally, then salt marsh may develop, colonised by various species of flowering plant such as cord grasses, *Spartina spp.*, Sea Purslane, *Halimione portulacoides*, and Sea Aster, *Aster tripolium*.

In general, difficulties of access and study make muddy shores less attractive to the seashore naturalist, though they have their own special charm and they are of particular interest for their winter bird-life.

Conserving the Seashore

Seas and seashores are under more threat today than ever before. Increasing numbers of people are able to go to coasts for their holidays, especially in the sunniest parts of the world, and this mass-migration is accompanied by major coastal developments. Steadily increasing boat traffic leads to increased oil spillage, more rubbish washing up on beaches and a rising level of pollution. All these factors, and many more, affect the quality of life in the seas and on beaches. Although many of these problems are global, over which we have very little control as individuals, it is always worth making your views known by reporting pollution incidents, contacting the Royal Society for the Prevention of Cruelty to Animals or the Royal Society for the Protection of Birds if you find live oiled birds, and by writing to local politicians if you believe that features of seashore life are threatened.

When looking at seashore life, it is important always to place the welfare of the organisms first; replace large stones where you find them, leave animals and plants where they are, or put them back when you have looked at them, and generally leave as few marks of your presence as you can.

Groups of Seashore Plants and Animals

The range of types of plants and animals occurring on the seashore is very wide and many will appear unfamiliar to those accustomed to terrestrial species. The following briefly introduces the groups covered, in the order in which they appear, with diagrams of the structures mentioned in the main text.

Plants

Algae

The algae are a group of simple, non-flowering plants that reproduce by spores. They are easily the most abundant of intertidal plants and come in a huge variety of forms. Very few are green, as most have additional pigments to allow them to absorb light under water. All algae have a simple structure, with no division into roots or leaves, though they may be highly divided. They are normally attached to the substrate by a holdfast, and they absorb all their food directly from sea water.

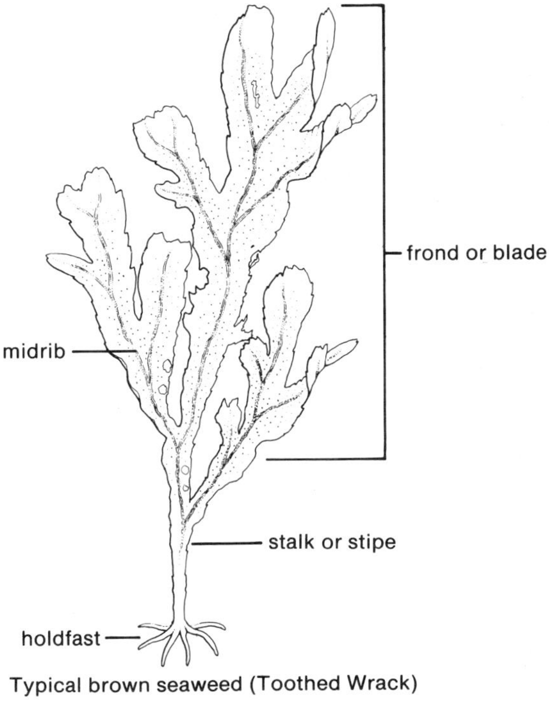

Typical brown seaweed (Toothed Wrack)

There are a few green species, such as Sea Lettuce, *Ulva lactuca*, though they form only a minor part of most communities. The most obvious species are usually the brown algae, which include the wracks, the kelps and various other species. Brown algae frequently dominate much of the shore. Less obvious, but often abundant, are the red algae. Generally they are small and not very conspicuous, and they vary from types that look almost like a red cabbage, through others that resemble sea-firs, to encrusting types that look more like lichens.

Flowering Plants

Flowering plants are more advanced than algae, particularly because of their more complex structure, and their ability to produce flowers and seeds. However, few have colonised the seashore, let alone the sea. One group of grasses, the eelgrasses, have adapted to genuine marine life, whilst a small selection of other flowering plants can withstand inundation at times.

Lichens

Lichens are extraordinary in that each species is a consistent association of two quite different plants – an alga and a fungus. They can survive in a wide range of conditions, including the seashore. Several species are abundant just above high-water mark, while a few have colonised the inundated parts of the shore.

Animal Life

Sponges (Porifera)

The sponges are simple primitive animals, lacking much specialisation of cells or structures. They consist basically of a chamber with a large opening, and they extract food and oxygen from the sea water that is drawn in through many smaller openings. They vary enormously in size, shape and colour, even within one species, and are notoriously difficult to identify.

Jellyfishes (Scyphozoa)

The jellyfishes are part of a larger group of organisms, the Cnidaria, which includes the sea-anemones and the Portuguese Man-o-war. In the jellyfishes, one particular phase of a complex life-cycle is dominant – this is the large, free-swimming creature, known as the medusa. This produces eggs and sperm that give rise to tiny polyps that attach themselves to a rock or other substrate. When they mature, these produce a series of small free-swimming medusae that eventually grow into 'jellyfishes'. They feed by catching prey with their long stinging tentacles. Apart from the small stalked jellyfishes, most are free-swimming, and are only found on the shore if they have been washed up.

Sea-anemones (Anthozoa)
Despite their name, the sea-anemones are animals, closely related to the jellyfishes. They are quite primitive and simple, with a bag-like chamber, into which the stinging tentacles push prey, though they also depend on planktonic animals that move in with sea water. Although the stinging tentacles can paralyse prey, they do not have any effect on humans. Sea-anemones occur in a wide variety of forms, mostly brightly coloured, with shapes that often resemble flowers.

Bristle Worms (Polychaeta)
These are part of the large group of segmented worms, and many of them look like more familiar terrestrial worms. They are enormously varied in structure, from the broad squat Sea Mouse, *Aphrodite aculeata*, to the tiny *Spirorbis* worm which hides away in coiled calcareous tubes on seaweed.

Molluscs (Mollusca)
The molluscs are a very large group of soft-bodied animals that almost always protect themselves in shells – all the animals normally referred to as sea shells are molluscs, except for barnacles,

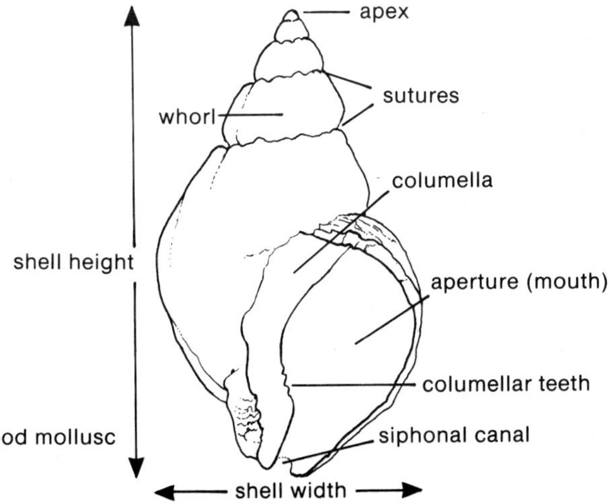

Gastropod mollusc

which are crustaceans. Because so many shells can be found on the shore, both live and washed up, this book features a large number of species. They are also relatively easy to identify, compared to most seashore organisms.

There are five main, distinct groups of molluscs found on our seashores; the chitons, the gastropods, the bivalves, the tusk shells (scaphopods) and the cephalopods, which are quite unlike other molluscs.

Bivalve mollusc

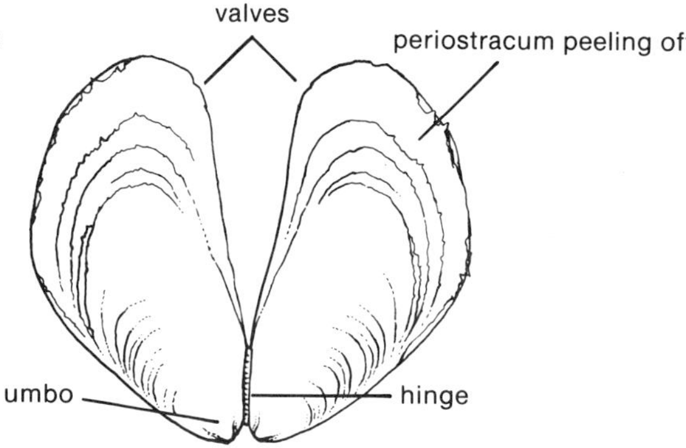

The chitons, or coat-of-mail shells, are inconspicuous creatures with a shell made up of calcareous plates, such that they look rather like a legless woodlouse.

The gastropods are the largest class of molluscs, with thousands of species. They are characterised by a single, often spiralled shell, except for the curious shell-less sea slugs. Gastropods include limpets, ormers, periwinkles, dogwhelks, and the sea-slug and its relatives.

The bivalves are molluscs in which the shell can be divided into two equal halves – they are bilaterally symmetrical. They are familiar in the form of mussels, cockles, razor shells and otter shells. In life, the valves of the shell are held shut when necessary by strong muscles, then opened to feed. Some species feed with the aid of a siphon, extracting food and oxygen from the moving stream of sea water. Many of the bivalves found on shores have been washed in from deeper water after death.

The scaphopods, or tusk shells, are a small specialised group of molluscs with elongated tusk-like shells, that live partly buried in sand or mud.

The cephalopods are superficially quite unlike other molluscs. They are mobile and predatory, with no external shell, and include the octopuses, cuttlefish and squid groups. Most are marine rather than shore animals, but the familiar cuttle-bone is the washed-up internal shell of dead cuttlefish.

Nudibranch mollusc (Sea Lemon)

Crustaceans (Crustacea)
The crustaceans are members of the huge phylum of arthropods (which includes the insects), and are more advanced than the

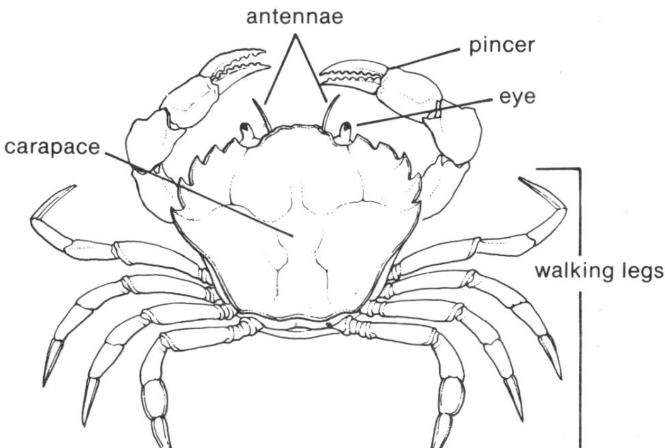

Typical crab (e.g. Common Shore Crab)

preceding groups, with a more complex body that has an external skeleton and a range of specialised tissue and organs. The crustaceans generally have a clearly defined head, thorax and abdomen, though the barnacles are rather different, and were only seen to be related to the crustaceans because of their very similar life history. Crabs, lobsters and prawns are more typical crustaceans, and they belong to the decapod order within crustaceans.

Insects (Insecta)
Very few insects have colonised the sea or seashore, despite the huge numbers of terrestrial species. Insects characteristically have a head; thorax and abdomen, with six legs, though this is not always apparent. The primitive springtails and bristle-tails are common on the seashore, together with more mobile species such as flies that scavenge when the tide is out.

Sea Spiders (Pycnogonida)
A small group of entirely marine arthropods, resembling terrestrial spiders, but not closely related, despite their possession of eight long legs.

Spiny-skinned Animals (Echinodermata)
This phylum includes the starfishes, the brittle stars, the feather stars and the sea-urchins. They are a distinctive, wholly marine, group with symmetrical bodies either spherical or disc-shaped as in the sea-urchins, or five-star-shaped (a form of symmetry known as pentamerism). Some groups are aggressively predatory, whilst others, such as most sea-urchins, browse on organic material on rocks.

Edible Sea-urchin

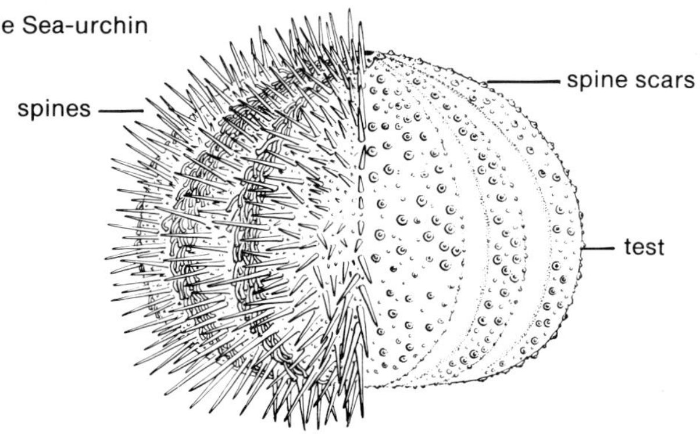

Rock Goby (underside)

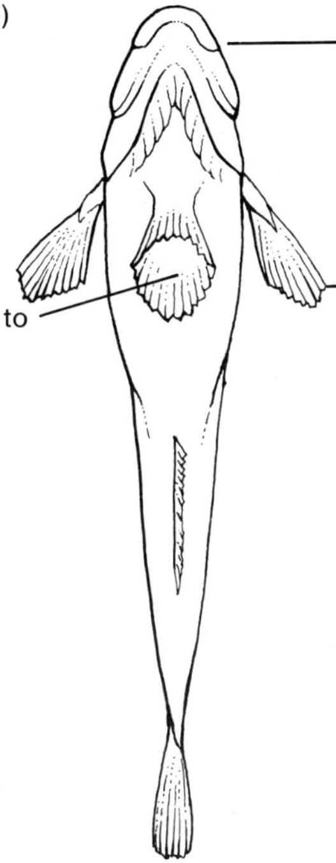

Bony Fishes (Osteichthyes)
These fishes form one group of the huge number of fishes. Relatively few occur on the seashore, though a number of smaller species, such as the gobies, are resident in rock pools, and other species may occasionally become stranded. Fishes that occur on the seashore are normally readily recognisable as such.

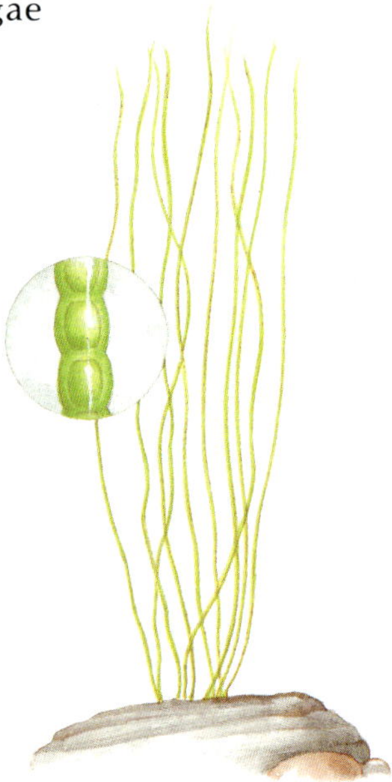

Green Hairweed *Chaetomorpha linum* A distinctive, though rather inconspicuous green seaweed, consisting of tufts of fine unbranched threads up to 30cm long. No obvious holdfast, but usually grows attached to a solid rocky base in a mass. The strands are soft rather than wiry; colour bright green. Very common in pools on the upper and middle shore, extending into fresher water, such as where a stream meets the sea. Most visible in spring and summer. Occurs widely throughout the Mediterranean, Atlantic, English Channel, North Sea and Baltic.

Grass Kelp *Enteromorpha intestinalis* Well-known and distinctive pale to bright green seaweed, notable for long unbranched cylindrical fronds which are inflated by gas-filled bubbles at intervals, thus resembling a section of gut. Fronds may reach 1m, though usually less. Frequently forms slippery masses on the upper shore, in varying situations, withstanding some degree of pollution, particularly if there are high nutrient levels. Especially common in estuaries. Most conspicuous in late winter/early spring when growth is strongest, dying and bleaching by late summer. Very common throughout all European seas. About 10 related species in the region.

Sea Lettuce *Ulva lactuca* An aptly named seaweed for its clusters of broad green leaf-like fronds, resembling miniature lettuces at times. Shape can vary widely, with leaves 10–50cm long. Fronds very bright green and translucent, sometimes with white patches where spores released; there is always a short stalk. Very abundant on rocky shores at lower levels, especially where nutrients are high (e.g. where there is sewage pollution). Visible throughout the year in milder areas. Occurs throughout Europe. Widely eaten. Several related species; it is similar to *Monostroma* which is funnel-shaped, not flattened.

Hen Pen *Bryopsis plumosa* A small but distinctive glossy green seaweed, with branched feathery fronds, arranged in one plane, and usually growing in tufts up to 12cm long. Also known as Sea-moss, for its resemblance to some mosses. Quite common on rocky shores, though inconspicuous and overlooked. Commonly grows in shadier parts of pools on the middle-lower shore, often under overhangs or amongst larger weeds. Most frequent and visible in spring and summer. Widespread throughout the whole region. Edible, though rather small. *Bryopsis hypnoides* is similar, but branched in all directions, not flattened.

Algae

Prasiola stipitata A small green seaweed, less than 3cm long, that usually grows in extensive slippery masses on the upper shore. Individual fronds are usually 1–2cm long, of which half is stalk and the remainder is oblong with curly edges, though variable according to habitat. It becomes conspicuous because it grows in quantity. Favoured habitat is rocks at the upper shore level, especially where nutrient levels are high or where there is slight pollution. Common throughout the Atlantic, English Channel and North Sea, but not Mediterranean. Similar to Sea Lettuce or *Enteromorpha linza*, but the long stalk is distinctive.

Cladophora rupestris Densely tufted, dark green seaweed, with masses of short, rather wiry fronds. Individual fronds up to 12cm long, usually irregularly branched, occasionally opposite. Appears less tufted when out of water, though this is easily checked by looking at the base of the plant. Grows on rocks or other solid substrates on middle to lower shore, especially underneath larger brown seaweeds such as wracks. Dies back in winter, though still visible, but most conspicuous in summer. Common throughout the Atlantic, English Channel, North Sea and Baltic. Similar species occur in the Mediterranean. Several other *Cladophora* species in region.

Velvet Horn *Codium tomentosum* The largest widespread green seaweed, with velvety tubular branched fronds. Commonly reaches about 40cm in length, more in deep water. Cylindrical fronds about 1cm in diameter, spongy in texture, with a regular branched pattern; usually yellowish-green. Holdfast is a mass of closely woven filaments, attached to rock. Occurs from the middle shore downwards into deep water; most often seen in lower shore rock pools, or washed up. Perennial, with maximum growth in winter. Found from the Mediterranean northwards to the English Channel, avoiding colder areas or low salinity. Several related species; none looks similar.

Monostroma grevillei Small, bright green seaweed, 10–20cm long, similar to Sea Lettuce but distinctly funnel-shaped with a split down one side. When out of water, it collapses to look less distinctive, but the shape can be readily seen on closer examination. The fronds are only one cell thick, whilst those of Sea Lettuce are two cells thick, though it takes practice to distinguish the two. Widespread in rock pools and on rock platforms from the lower middle shore downwards into shallow water. Occurs in the Atlantic, English Channel, North Sea and Baltic, but not the Mediterranean. Several similar species occur.

Leathesia difformis This brown seaweed consists of strange-looking, olive-brown rounded knobbly lumps, 2–5cm in diameter, growing on rocks and other seaweeds. The lumps are solid when young, becoming hollow as they age, with the thin branching filaments visible inside. Occurs on the middle and lower shore levels. First appears in the spring, becomes very common by midsummer, disappearing by the autumn. Widely distributed in the Atlantic, English Channel and North Sea. A similar species is the Oyster Thief (*Colpomenia peregrina*) which grows attached to seaweeds and shells, but is dry and papery, not jelly-like.

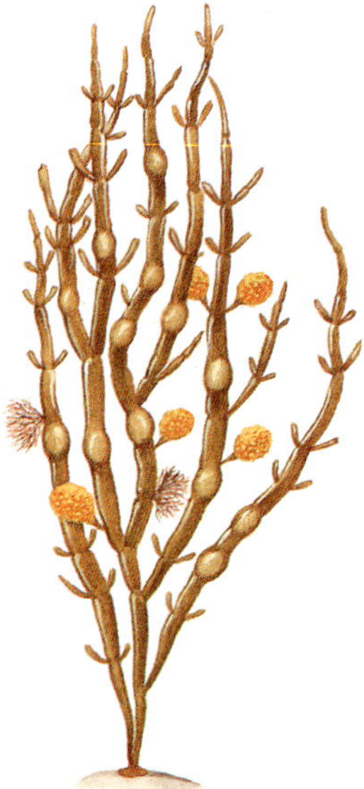

Knotted Wrack *Ascophyllum nodosum* Untidy brown seaweed, with egg-shaped bladders along the stems. The bladders do not 'pop' like those of Bladderwrack, and in other respects they look quite different. Fronds up to 1.5m long, branching repeatedly and unevenly. There are separate male and female plants, with each producing raisin-like fruiting bodies, yellow in the male, greenish in the female. A very common species of sheltered rocky shores, blanketing the rocks in the right conditions, though very stunted where exposure is too great. Occurs throughout the Atlantic, English Channel and North Sea.

Bootlace Weed *Chorda filum* Very distinctive brown seaweed looking, as its name suggests, like long bootlaces. Fronds only 5–6mm in diameter, but may grow up to 8m long in favourable conditions; unbranched and slimy, but surprisingly strong. Adult plants become hollow with air bladders. Frequently found washed up in coiled masses, though mainly grows below low water mark. Common on rocky and gravelly shores, in calmer places. Annual, reaching maximum growth in late summer. Occurs throughout the Atlantic, English Channel, North Sea and Baltic. *Chordaria flagelliformis* and Thongweed (*Himanthalia elongata*) are similar but branched.

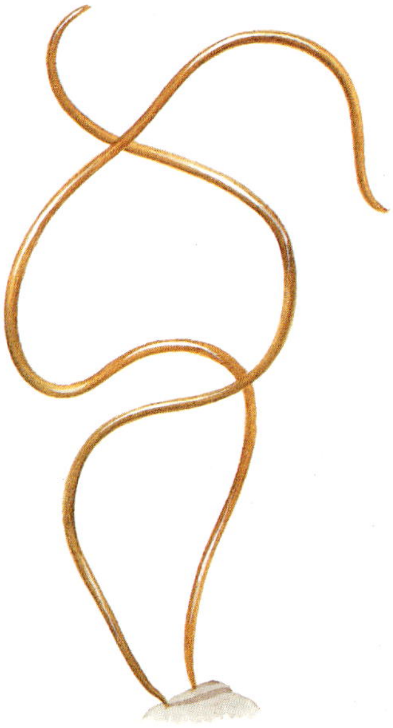

Maiden's Hair *Ectocarpus siliculosus* A small untidy-looking seaweed consisting of masses of fine tangled branches, becoming free towards the ends. The fronds grow to about 30cm long and are yellow-brown to green-brown. Grows commonly on rocks, smaller stones and other seaweeds, from the middle shore down into shallow water, though it is often overlooked. Occurs in the Mediterranean, Atlantic, English Channel, North Sea and Baltic, though not in the coldest parts. There are many species of *Ectocarpus*, distinctive enough as a group, but very hard to separate from one another.

Beanweed *Scytosiphon lomentaria* Seaweed that somewhat resembles a long narrow string of greenish, slimy sausages. Fronds up to 30cm in length; tubular and unbranched with gas-bladders at intervals, divided by constrictions; greenish or yellowish-brown. It is very common, often abundant, on rocky and stony shores, growing on all kinds of substrates from the middle shore down into shallow water. Most conspicuous in winter, except in the coldest areas. Occurs throughout the region, from the Mediterranean to the Baltic and Atlantic. Edible, and apparently tasting of beans – hence the name. Unlikely to be confused with much else.

Bladderwrack *Fucus vesiculosus* Probably the best-known of all seaweeds, particularly noted for its poppable bladders. The fronds consist of regularly branched flattened blades, up to 1m long, with 2 or 3 bladders on each branch; the swollen, soft, knobbly reproductive organs on the branch tips tend to be yellowish in male plants, greenish in female plants. Very common and widespread on rocky shores, growing in a distinct zone on the middle shore, but not on very exposed sites. Occurs throughout colder water areas in the Atlantic, English Channel, North Sea and Baltic. A similar species in the Mediterranean, *F. virosoides*, has no bladders.

Toothed Wrack *Fucus serratus*
A typical greenish-brown wrack, recognisable by the toothed edges to its fronds, and the lack of any bladders. The fronds grow to about 60cm long, occasionally more, and they generally have a distinct greenish tinge to the brown colour. They are irregularly branched, flattened, and rather uneven in width. Occurs, often abundantly, in a distinct zone on the lower to middle section of rocky shores, with only short exposure to air. It provides homes and shelter for numerous other species. Widespread throughout colder water areas in the Atlantic, English Channel, North Sea and Baltic.

Spiral Wrack *Fucus spiralis*
A typical brown wrack, rather similar to Bladderwrack but distinguished by its twisted fronds, lack of bladders, and conspicuous reproductive bodies. The branched, twisted fronds reach 40cm long and are greenish-brown, sometimes yellowish. The midrib is strongly marked, and the tips of the branches are swollen with reproductive organs, which do not quite reach the edge of the frond and are surrounded by a strip of flat blade. It is a common species on the upper zone of rocky shores, away from exposed areas. Occurs throughout northern parts, absent from the Mediterranean.

Fucus ceranoides An undistinguished wrack, with regularly branched fronds and clusters of small, branched reproductive bodies at the tips. The greenish-brown fronds reach 60cm and are usually smaller than other wracks. Most common in brackish water, rather than strongly salty water, such as in estuaries, where it grows on rock, stones and gravel at all shore levels. Frequent, but often missed. Occurs in the Atlantic, English Channel and North Sea. Could be confused with poor specimens of other wracks, and similar in form to Channelled Wrack, though differentiated by its strong midrib and lack of channels.

Bifurcaria bifurcata A brown seaweed, rather similar to a wrack. The tubular fronds reach about 60cm; they are unbranched for the lower quarter but repeatedly forked above this, ending in much-branched tips, some of which may bear swollen, long-oval reproductive organs. It occurs on rock and in rock pools on the lower shore, but is not normally found exposed to the air (unlike the wracks). Primarily an Atlantic species, occurring round south and south-west Britain. It has no immediate relatives.

Sea Sorrel *Desmarestia ligulata*
Belongs to a group of much-branched, fern-like species. The numerous branched fronds, up to 1.5m and roughly triangular in outline, are carried on a central stem; they are tufted with fine hairs in summer; olive brown when alive and submerged, but soon turning green and flabby out of water. Often washed up. Contains sulphuric acid and tends to bleach other seaweeds growing next to it. Found on rocky shores and in pools, from lower shore into shallow water. Occurs in the Atlantic and English Channel. Several similar related species, such as *D. aculeata* and *D. viridis*.

Sea Oak *Halidrys siliquosa*
A much-branched, robust brown seaweed. Fronds up to 1m long, with numerous uneven branches; stiff and leathery in texture; slightly greenish. The air bladders on the ends of the branches are divided internally into chambers and resemble seed-pods of the mustard family; the largest bladders have long sharp points. Occurs on rocks on the lower shore and in shallow water, extending higher up the shore in sheltered places. Widespread through the Atlantic, English Channel and North Sea, though rarely common. Superficially similar to seaweeds such as *Bifurcaria* though the bladders are quite different.

Cytoseira tamariscifolia A bushy, spiky, untidy seaweed that resembles the branched foliage of tamarisk. Fronds are 30–40cm long, olive-brown, with numerous branches, and short spiky projections along the main stem; small air bladders and tufts of reproductive organs are carried towards the tips. Seen underwater, the fronds appear iridescent. Common on rocks and in pools, from the lower shore down into shallow water, becoming rarer further north. Widespread through the Mediterranean, Atlantic and English Channel. There are many similar species of *Cytoseira*, with different branching patterns.

Kelp, Oarweed or **Tangle** *Laminaria digitata* Familiar, large brown seaweed, consisting of a strong stalk and a broad fan-like blade made up of numerous strap-like sections. Size ranges from about 1m up to 3–4m. Stalk flexible, oval in cross-section. Grows in masses at lowest tidal level and below on rocky shores, with 'forests' of it exposed at lowest tides. Common and widespread throughout cooler waters: Atlantic, English Channel, North Sea and Baltic. Similar to *L. hyperborea*, which has a rougher stalk, and Furbelows (*Saccorhiza polyschides*), whose stalk has uneven edges and bulbous outgrowths. Both these species live in deeper water.

Sugar Kelp *Laminaria saccharina*
Distinctive and familiar seaweed, consisting of a single, long belt-like frond. It is yellowish-brown to pure brown, with a short stalk that widens into a convoluted blade, up to 3m long in total. When dry, crystals of a sugary substance, mannitol, are visible on its surface. Common on rockier shores, where it grows attached to various solid objects, from lowest shore downwards, though often washed up. A species of cold, clear waters in the Atlantic, English Channel and North Sea. Unlike any other common species when mature.

Furbelows *Saccorhiza polyschides*
A massive brown seaweed, with a long uneven stalk and a broad fan of strap-like blades, arising from a yellowish knobbly holdfast that looks as though it is made from rubber. Similar to Kelp but generally larger, up to 4m, and distinguished by holdfast and knobbly, wavy-edged stalk. Usually grows in deeper water than Kelp (though annual, and often washed up after late autumn gales); more frequently found in small quantities rather than 'forests'. Widespread and frequent on rocky shores at the lowest levels all around Britain, in the Atlantic, English Channel and North Sea.

Dabberlocks *Alaria esculenta* A long, strap-like brown seaweed, with a blade up to 2m or more long, and a distinctive midrib along the whole length. The frond is more delicate and often greener than the kelps, which lack the midrib. It often becomes torn and tattered after rough weather. On the short basal stalk, there are groups of lobe-shaped leaves, known as sporophylls, which bear the reproductive organs. Grows commonly on exposed rocky shores, surviving heavy wave-battering, despite its delicate appearance. A cold-water species, occurring in the North Sea and on northern Atlantic coasts.

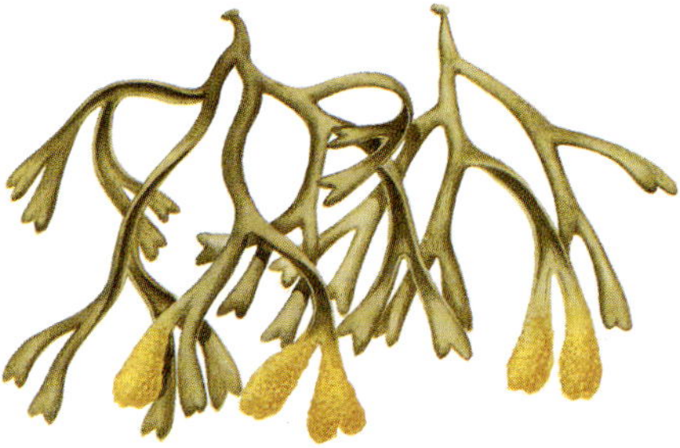

Channelled Wrack *Pelvetia canaliculata* A brown wrack with markedly grooved fronds. Although this species is similar in colour and general form to the *Fucus* wracks, close examination reveals that the fronds are curled over, forming a channel that usually lies *facing* the rock surface. The fronds are short, to about 15cm long, and the tips may be swollen with typical wrack reproductive organs. It is a very common species, forming a distinct zone on the upper parts of rocky shores, even extending above high water mark. Occurs throughout the Atlantic, English Channel and North Sea.

Peacock's Tail *Padina pavonia* An unusual little species, consisting of robust, silvery, fan-shaped upright fronds, with a greenish tinge inside and brown stripes outside. The individual fronds are triangular in form, narrowing down to the holdfast, but maintaining a roughly funnel-shaped structure normally 5–10cm high. Widespread, though rarely common, on rocky shores, in shallow water and in rock pools on the lower shore. A warmer water species, found from the southern coasts of Britain southwards to the Mediterranean. No very close species.

Punctaria latifolia This seaweed consists of simple undivided blades, up to 40cm long, with very short stalks. The blades are about 7–8cm across, distinctly greenish in colour with darker spots and hairs; they may be blunt or pointed at the tip. Widespread on rocks, stones and shells, including live limpets, from the middle shore down into shallow water. Occurs throughout the region, except in the Baltic. Similar species include *Petalonia fasciata* which is smaller and unspotted, and occurs mainly in mid-winter; *Punctaria plantaginea* which is smaller and narrower; and the tiny *P. tenuissima*, with almost grass-like thin fronds.

Sargassum vulgare A rather atypical brown seaweed, appearing more like a flowering plant than an alga, due to its combination of branches with leaf-like fronds and berry-like bladders. Fronds up to 30cm long, branch irregularly and carry blade-shaped 'leaves', some of which bear bladders. There are also small branched reproductive organs amongst the fronds. Occurs on rocky and stony beaches in the Mediterranean area from low water down to considerable depths. Several similar species in the Mediterranean area include *S. linifolium*, with narrower fronds, and *S. hornschuchi*, which is larger and longer, with more crinkled fronds.

Japweed *Sargassum muticum* Recognisable by its enormous length, though otherwise typical of *Sargassum* species. The fronds can reach 5m long, and if a section is pulled tightly, the branches will hang down evenly like washing on a line. Only relatively recently found in Britain, as a coloniser from Japan, on the south coast. It has subsequently spread rapidly, especially westwards, and can become very abundant in sheltered areas. There is no other species like it in British waters. Fears have been expressed that its great length, and ability to colonise shallow muddy harbour waters, may cause fouling problems in anchorages.

Thongweed *Himanthalia elongata*
The long, branched, narrow strap-shaped fronds of this seaweed arise from small toadstool-shaped structures surmounting the holdfast. The fronds may be up to 2m long, branching evenly though only by a limited amount. The curious olive-green 'toadstool' structures may often be found without the main frond. A common species on exposed rocky shores, from the lower shore downwards into shallow water, and in rock pools. Occurs in the Atlantic and English Channel only. Somewhat similar to Bootlace Weed, though this species is unbranched, cylindrical, and lacking the 'toadstools'.

Laver *Porphyra umbilicalis*
A well-known edible seaweed, most distinctive when seen growing in slimy leafy extensive masses over the rocks. Individual fronds can be hard to distinguish from the mass; they are delicate and membranous, up to 20cm long, lobed like leaves and forming irregular groups; reddish-purple when growing strongly. Locally common on exposed beaches which are both sandy and rocky. Occurs in the Mediterranean, Atlantic, English Channel and North Sea. Eaten as a delicacy, especially in Wales. There are several related and similar species of *Porphyra*, all edible.

Landlady's Wig *Ahnfeltia plicata* A wiry tufted species, consisting of clusters of dark red fronds. The texture of this plant has been described as being 'like a lump of 2-amp fuse wire', and differentiates it from similar-looking species. The fronds are much-branched, in tufts that are about 10cm across and 15cm high, of such dark red that they are nearly black. Occurs in rock pools and on rocky shores from the middle shore downwards into shallow water. Widely distributed and common locally in the Atlantic, English Channel and North Sea. No closely related species.

Irish Moss or **Carragheen** *Chondrus crispus* A delicate red-purple species, reminiscent of some forms of salad lettuce. The frond is regularly divided to form a much-branched structure, but the resulting blades are usually broad and flat, without midribs or inrolled margins. The lower part of the blade is a short, unbranched 'stem', and the whole frond reaches about 15cm long. Common and widespread on lower rocky shores, in shallow water, and occasionally in pools. Widely used as a food and a gelling agent. Occurs in the Atlantic, English Channel and North Sea; rare in the Baltic. Similar to *Gigartina stellata*.

Sea Noodle *Nemalion helminthoides* A strange red seaweed, looking very like a cluster of curly spaghetti. The individual fronds are cylindrical, slimy and worm-like, about 2cm in diameter and up to 25cm long. Some forms just branch once at the base, other forms branch throughout their length. They vary in colour from red to purplish-brown. Locally common on the lower shore and in rock pools, on exposed rocky shores. Occurs mainly in the Atlantic, but infrequent in the North Sea, and rare in the Baltic. No other similar species.

Dulse *Rhodymenia palmata* A rather amorphous alga, consisting of a cluster of broad, flat divided blades. The individual fronds are broad, flat and thick, widening out from a very short or non-existent stalk, reaching 20-30cm in length, and red-crimson in colour. Occurs commonly, mainly on rocky shores, attached to rocks, stones and large seaweeds, especially *Laminaria*. Widespread in the Atlantic, English Channel and North Sea. Related species occur in the Mediterranean. It is well known as an edible and medicinal species. Can be confused with *Dilsea carnosa*, which has a longer stalk.

Delesseria sanguinea Resembles a bunch of reddish leaves fallen from a tree. The frond consists of a short main stem, dividing into a number of leaf-like branches, each with midribs and side veins, and wavy margins; the whole structure can reach 30–40cm in length, bright translucent red. The fronds disintegrate late in the year, and small spore-bearing outgrowths develop along the midrib. Common on rocks and larger seaweeds in the lower shore, mainly in deep shady pools, where it occurs as isolated plants. Found throughout the Atlantic, English Channel and North Sea; rare in the Baltic.

Gigartina stellata A red alga very similar to Irish Moss. The fronds of this species are up to 20cm in length; broad, flat and regularly divided, but the margins of the fronds are inrolled, giving a channelled appearance, and older specimens are dotted with pimples. Abundant on rocky shores, sometimes forming a band at the lower level. Widespread throughout the Atlantic, English Channel and North Sea, commonest in the west. Edible, and used with or in place of Irish Moss. Related species of *Gigartina* occur.

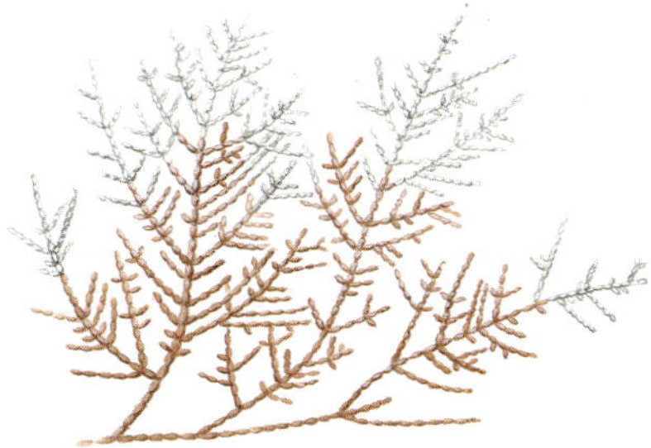

Corallina officinalis Fern-like red seaweed, with calcified fronds that turn white as they die. The individual fronds reach 8–12cm in length and are notable for their regular branching, every branch or branchlet having an exact opposite. The main branches are made up of tiny articulated sections. The original reddish-plum colour fades as the plant ages, or is exposed to the sun, turning yellow then white. Common on the middle shore, particularly as a fringe around rock pools just below water level. Widespread throughout the Mediterranean, Atlantic, English Channel and North Sea; rare in the Baltic. Several other *Corallina* species occur.

Pepper Dulse *Laurencia pinnatifida* An attractive, but small and inconspicuous alga. The individual fronds, commonly up to 12cm long or occasionally more, have a strong main stem, divided on either side into branches like the rungs of a ladder, which are further divided into finer tufts at the ends; they are reddish to yellowish-brown. Grows in clusters on rocks and in crevices from the middle shore downwards into shallow water. Widespread and locally common throughout the Mediterranean, Atlantic, English Channel and North Sea. Related species of *Laurencia* with different branching patterns occur.

Eelgrass e.g. *Zostera angustifolia* A grass-like flowering plant that has become totally marine. The eelgrasses have leaves typical of grasses and their relatives, i.e. long and thin, up to 1m, with a series of parallel veins. There are separate male and female plants, each producing different flowers. Two species (*Z. angustifolia* and *Z. noltii*) occur mainly in the sheltered waters of estuaries from mid shore down to shallow water; a third species (*Z. marina*) grows on muddy and sandy beaches from lowest tide levels down to about 4m, and is thus rarely seen. All flower from mid to late summer. Found throughout Europe.

Sea Purslane *Halimione portulacoides* A small flowering evergreen shrub, 30–80cm high, with greyish mealy leaves. The flowers are individually insignificant, but the orange-green spikes are noticeable *en masse* from June–September. Occurs commonly around the top of salt marshes and along creeks, often forming a distinct zone. It is also know as 'crab-grass', since it is well known as a hiding place for crabs. Common and often abundant in suitable sheltered sites throughout Europe.

Cord Grass *Spartina anglica*
Stout, erect grass that may cover vast areas in sheltered estuaries and bays. Tall wheat-like, flowering spikes up to 1m or more, produced June–August. Arose as a hybrid between two other *Spartina* species, but now accepted as a species itself. More aggressive than its parents, and colonises further into deeper water, often ousting more demanding salt-marsh species. Widely used as a mud-binder to reclaim tidal land, which it raises by trapping silt. Widespread and common in most areas; often introduced. The two original species, *S. maritima* and *S. alternifolia* are both slenderer and rarer.

Glasswort or **Marsh Samphire**
Salicornia sp An erect flowering plant, with shiny, succulent jointed stems that bear numerous shorter side branches all round. Individual plants are usually 20–30cm high, depending upon the species and the situation. Annual, bright green for much of the summer and becoming reddish and woody before dying back completely by late autumn. Grows in extensive masses on mudflats, salt marshes and estuaries. *S. europaea* is the commonest of a whole group of similar related species, which collectively occur in suitable coastal habitats throughout Europe.

Verrucaria maura A black or greenish-black encrusting lichen that occurs on rocks in irregularly circular patches. On close examination, the body of the lichen can be seen to be cracked into roughly rectangular sections, sometimes with small conical fruiting bodies. The crust is very thin. Extensive patches are often taken for dried-up oil washed up from ships. Very common on rocky coasts from above high water to some way below it, usually occurring just below the distinctive orange lichen zone. Found in suitable habitats around Atlantic, English Channel and North Sea coasts.

Verrucaria mucosa Usually greenish-grey to olive-green lichen, the crust of which attaches very closely to the rock. Very similar to *V. maura* but the crust is slightly thicker and not cracked into rectangular sections. It occurs in irregular patches on rocks, but only on those *below* high water mark. Common on Atlantic and English Channel coasts. Similar species include *V. microspora* and *V. striatula*, which have a similar distribution, and *V. adriatica*, which occurs in similar habitats in the Mediterranean area.

Lichina pygmaea An upright, branching lichen, only about 1cm high, forming small bushes like a miniature seaweed. It occurs in tiny patches, up to a few centimetres across, made up of dark brown to black, much-divided branches. It is common in suitable habitats on rocky shores from high water mark downwards, so it is regularly immersed. It occurs on Mediterranean, Atlantic and English Channel coasts. Similar species include *L. confinis* which is smaller (less than 5mm high) and even more branched; it is common on rocks over a similar area.

Sulphur Sponge or **Sea Orange** *Suberites domuncula* A fleshy, globular orange-yellow sponge. Very variable, but most commonly roughly spherical, up to 30cm diameter, with a smooth surface, and fleshy and elastic in texture. If removed from water, it shrinks rapidly. It occurs in clean water from low water mark downwards, on rocks, harbour piles etc, and has a particular association with whelk shells occupied by hermit crabs. May eventually dissolve away the shell and form the crab's home directly. Distributed throughout the Mediterranean, Atlantic, English Channel and North Sea. *S. cavernosus*, a Mediterranean species, is similar, though often stalked.

Breadcrumb Sponge *Halichondria panicea* Resembles a section of the moon's surface. The encrusting body varies from white, through orange, to green, depending partly on the degree of colonisation of algae, which relates to the light levels. Occurs in irregular rounded areas up to 20–25cm across, usually with characteristic 'craters', but occasionally with more elongated structures. Colonises rock surfaces, stones, and larger seaweeds from the middle shore down into deep water. Common and widespread in the Mediterranean, Atlantic, English Channel, North Sea and parts of the Baltic. *Oscarella lobularis* is similar, but smaller and orangey-pink.

Common Jellyfish *Aurelia aurita* A typical jellyfish, most commonly seen as a dome of transparent jelly washed up on the shore. In this species, the 'umbrella' is circular with a diameter of about 25cm, and there are 4 conspicious, long, purplish mouth-arms hanging below. The purple crescent-shaped reproductive organs are visible within the umbrella. A pelagic floating species that occurs virtually throughout the world, becoming washed up on the beaches according to tides and gales. Large groups may often be found together. *Cyanea lamarckii* is similar, but with the margin extended into frilly lobes.

Beadlet Anemone *Actinia equina* The common 'sea-anemone', familiar both as a closed blob, or open with waving tentacles. When open under water, it is about 5-6cm in diameter and up to 7cm high, with hundreds of tentacles arranged in rings. When disturbed, or out of water, the tentacles can be quickly retracted, and the animal reverts to a blob of jelly about 3cm high. Colour variable, most commonly red-orange, but also green or brown; strawberry form is red with yellowish spots. Very common on rocky shores from middle shore downwards. Widespread throughout Mediterranean, Atlantic, English Channel and North Sea.

Snakelocks Anemone *Anemonia sulcata* This attractive anemone has a mass of long colourful tentacles that almost hide the short broad trunk. The tentacles may be up to 12cm long, occasionally more, and are not fully retractable; most commonly green tipped with pink-purple though various other colours occur. Common in clear rocky conditions, from pools on the middle shore downwards, though thriving best in well-lit situations. A southern and western species, found on the Mediterranean, Atlantic coasts and western English Channel. A distinctive species, unlikely to be confused.

Green Leaf Worm *Eulalia viridis* An attractive and conspicuous long, thin, slow-moving green worm with paddle-like legs. The body may be made up of 50–200 segments, with a total length of up to 15cm, more commonly 10cm; bright grass-green. Commonly seen creeping around on rocks at low tide, especially in dull weather, stretching and contracting slowly. Also lives, often unseen, in rock crevices. Common in the Mediterranean, Atlantic, English Channel, North Sea and western Baltic. The King Rag Worm (*Nereis virens*) has similar colour and leg shape, but this predatory species is usually much larger.

Spirorbis borealis Tiny coiled calcareous shells on seaweeds that look more like molluscs than worms. When under water, the green tentacles of the worms can be seen; the rest of the time, they simply appear as immobile *clockwise*-coiled tubes (as viewed from above), which are white and 3–5mm across. Very common, often extremely abundant, on the middle and lower shore on brown seaweeds such as the kelps and wracks, also on rocks and stones. Occurs in the Mediterranean, Atlantic, English Channel and North Sea. There are other similar species.

Coat-of-mail Chiton
Lepidopleurus asellus A small articulated mollusc, resembling a legless woodlouse. Consists of jointed shells, made up of 8 sections, reaching up to 2cm long overall; usually brown, with same-colour margin. Found attached to rocks, stones and other hard surfaces from the lower shore down into considerable depths of water. Widespread and common, though easily overlooked, in the Atlantic, English Channel and North Sea. Many other species; identification depends particularly on colour, whether margin and jointed section are the same colour, and ratio of total width to width of articulated section.

Common Ormer *Haliotis lamellosa* A large ear-shaped shell, with a line of holes along one edge. It is roughly oval, up to about 7cm long and 4cm across. The upper surface is creased, folded and ridged, and often encrusted with calcareous algae; colour variable, from brown to green, depending partly on the amount of algal encrustation. The inside is thickly covered with beautiful mother-of-pearl. Occurs on rocks or under stones from the lower shore down into shallow water. Widespread and common in the Mediterranean, but not elsewhere. Likely to be confused with the Green Ormer (*H. tuberculata*).

Green Ormer *Haliotis tuberculata* A large greenish ear-shaped shell. Very similar in shape to the Common Ormer, but larger (up to 10cm), with much less marked ridges and grooves; not normally encrusted with algae. There is a line of holes along one edge of the shell, with further older ones blocked off. Inside thickly lined with mother-of-pearl. Occurs on lower shore and into shallow water, strongly attached to rocks and stones. Found in Mediterranean, and Atlantic as far north as the Channel Isles, where it is a well-known food source.

Slit Limpet *Eumarginula reticulata* A distinctive triangular or conical shell, with a slightly turned-over tip and a marked slit down one side. It is about 2–3cm high, strongly ribbed, white or cream. Occurs on rocks and stones from the lower shore down into deep water. Widespread, though not especially common, in the Mediterranean, Atlantic, English Channel and North Sea. Several similar species occur, including *E. elongata* which is smaller, yellower and more turned over at the apex; and *E. cancellata*, which has lines of small tubercles radiating down from the tip.

Keyhole Limpet *Diodora apertura* One of a small group of limpets with typical conical shells that have a rectangular or rounded opening at the apex. Elongated when seen from above, 3–4cm long; yellowish or creamy-grey outside; regularly ribbed from the apex; has a clearly visible 'keyhole', through which a small tube protrudes when the animal is alive and under water. Fairly common on rocks from the lower shore downwards into moderately deep water. Occurs in the Atlantic, English Channel and North Sea. A similar species, *D. italica*, found in the Mediterranean, is more grey-blue in colour, with stronger stripes.

Tortoiseshell Limpet *Acmaea (Collisella) tessulata* A typically shaped limpet, with a distinctive tortoiseshell marbling on its outer surface. The shell is conical, slightly flattened, about 20–30cm high, with strong reddish-brown and white markings. Inside the shell, the apex is brown. More delicate than the Common Limpet and easily recognised. Common on rocks and stones from the lower shore down into deep water. Only occurs in northern parts of the region: northern Atlantic coasts, North Sea and Baltic. The White Tortoiseshell Limpet (*Acmaea virginea*) is much smaller, paler and less mottled, though otherwise similar.

Common Limpet *Patella vulgata* Well-known and abundant species. The conical shell is up to 7cm long, the largest limpet in the area; irregularly but not strongly ribbed, and usually pale cream or grey, not boldly marked. Often encrusted with barnacles. The interior is creamy to yellowish, with a silvery-brown scar at the apex. Very common on rocky shores from the upper shore downwards, becoming smaller and flatter further down. Occurs throughout the Atlantic, English Channel and North Sea. A number of similar species occur, including China limpet (*P. aspera*) which has a bluish interior with orange headscar.

Blue-rayed Limpet *Patina (Helcion) pellucida* A beautiful little limpet, with strongly marked electric-blue rays across its shell. Up to about 2cm long, oval or pear-shaped when seen from above, low and rounded from the side. The distinctive radiating lines of bright blue dots usually emanate from a dark blue spot at the narrower end. Variable in size and colour according to age. Almost invariably found attached to *Laminaria* kelp seaweeds, rather than rocks, from the lower shore down into moderately deep water. Common throughout most of the Atlantic, English Channel and North Sea area.

Toothed Winkle or **Thick Topshell** *Monodonta lineata* A pointed coiled shell, about 2–3cm high, and a similar width. Conical with 6 whorls, though these may be difficult to interpret. Tip usually white or grey; remainder of external surface has zig-zag markings in reddish-purple, occasionally green, or mixed. Mouth has a single projecting tooth in the otherwise smooth lines. Inside strongly coated with mother-of-pearl. Occurs on rocks of the middle shore. Locally very common in the Atlantic as far north as North Wales, and as far west as central English Channel. *M. turbinata* similar, but flatter, darker, with less marked tooth, occurring in the Mediterranean only.

Flat or **Purple Topshell** *Gibbula umbilicalis* A small conical, coiled shell, about 1–1.5cm high, with distinctly flattened apex, and up to 2cm across. There are usually 7 whorls in all. It is silvery green-grey, with strongly marked red-purple 'pyjama' stripes radiating out from the apex down to the mouth. It occurs on rocks and stones from the upper shore down to the lower shore; locally abundant. An Atlantic and English Channel species, but primarily south-western. Several other topshells occur, such as *G. magus*, the Grey Topshell (*G. cineraria*) and the Mediterranean *Monodonta turbinata*.

Common or **Painted Topshell** *Calliostoma zizyphinum* A beautiful conical shell, about 2.5–3cm high, with a maximum width of 3cm. The sides are very straight, with little distinction between the coils. Surface yellowish-pink, with darker mottling and pronounced darker dotted stripes spiralling around the shell; also occurs in white and violet-blue forms. Widely distributed and common on the lower shore and downwards into deep water. Occurs in the Mediterranean, Atlantic, English Channel and North Sea. The Grooved Topshell (*Cantharidus striatus*) is like a much smaller version, 1cm high and narrower across.

Rough Star Shell *Astraea rugosa* A strikingly attractive shell, conical in outline but very strongly ridged, with many projections. It is large, up to 5cm high and slightly wider across the widest part, rough and bulky in appearance. There are 7 whorls, though they are difficult to distinguish fully. The surface is heavily moulded into spikes and ridges, usually reddish-brown in colour, occasionally greyer. Occurs on rocks from the lower shore down into deeper water. A southern species, found in the Mediterranean, and Atlantic around Spain and Portugal only. No similar species.

Flat Periwinkle *Littorina littoralis* A common and variable shell, rounded in outline and with a flat top. Small, barely reaching 1cm high, and about the same across, and distinctly compressed downwards so the mouth reaches almost to the apex. Shell surface smooth; usually orange, but also occurs in brown, red, green and occasionally striped forms. Most frequently found moving over the surface of brown seaweeds, especially wracks, on which it grazes; active out of the water, unlike many species. Sometimes abundant on the middle shore. Occurs in the Atlantic, English Channel, North Sea and western Baltic.

Rough Periwinkle *Littorina saxatilis* A variable conical shell, with a pointed apex and a rough stripy surface. It is 1-1.25cm high, markedly coiled, with 6-9 coils separated by distinct grooves. The curve of the shell opening meets the main spire at a right angle. Colour variable, but usually orange-red to black, though often appearing rather grey and faded. The shell is distinctly rough to the touch. It feeds on seaweeds, and can breathe in air, like the Flat Periwinkle. Usually found on rocks, though when the tide is out, on upper and middle shore. Widespread throughout the region.

Edible Periwinkle *Littorina littorea* A large solid and robust periwinkle, up to 3cm high, with a pointed conical shape. Colour variable from red, through grey to black, usually rather dull, though always with some concentric darker striping. Often has bands and apex of different colour. Surface slightly rough to the touch. Small individuals distinguishable from Rough Periwinkle by the narrower angle at which the edge of the opening meets the spire. Common from middle tidal level down; active in air. Widespread throughout the region. Confusable with Dogwhelk (*Nucella lapillus*) which has a narrower opening, and is less striped or banded.

Laver Spire Shell *Hydrobia ulvae* A small, thinly conical shell, with 6 distinct narrow whorls. Rather undistinguished, about 0.6cm high, and much narrower across the base. The apex is bluntly pointed. Most commonly yellowish-brown, though variable. A very abundant species in salt marshes and estuarine mudflats, extending from middle shore level into quite brackish (i.e. less salty) areas. Grazes on Sea Lettuce. Widespread throughout the Atlantic, English Channel, North Sea and Baltic. *H. ventrosa* is similar, but with whorl sections more inflated looking, and point sharper.

Tower Shell *Turritella communis* Also known as the 'screw shell' because of its long, tapering whorled shape. Tall and thin, up to 6cm high, but only about 1cm across, with up to 19 distinct whorls. Each lower whorl has 3 or so further ridges. Aperture rounded. Variable in colour from near-white, through red to brown. Frequently abundant at some depth in muddy gravel beaches, though often washed up when empty. Common in the Mediterranean, Atlantic, English Channel and North Sea. *T. triplicata* is similar, but has less marked whorls, and is found only in the Mediterranean.

Common Cerith *Cerithium vulgatum* A distinctive, tall spire shell, with a strongly sculptured surface. It is about 6cm tall, but very narrow, with some 10 or 11 distinct whorls, with well-marked troughs between each, and regular projections and sculpturing around the whorls. Mouth oval, with a prominent tooth on each side. Colour is greyish or black, occasionally reddish or brown. Occurs among stones and in muddy sand from low tide down to 10m deep. Found in the Mediterranean only. The Rock Cerith (*C. rupestre*) is smaller and less markedly spiralled; Mediterranean only.

Pelican's Foot Shell *Aporrhais pespelecani* Resembles a tower shell except that the edges of the aperture are drawn out into 4 massive pointed fins. Height 4–5cm; has about 9 well-marked whorls, each with a line of raised pointed knobs. In mature specimens, the projections from the edge of the aperture are almost as long as the spire. Colour variable, from pinkish-grey or yellowish-grey, to brown or even black. A deep-water species, not normally found living on the shore, though occasionally washed up and often dredged up. Common in the Mediterranean, Atlantic, English Channel and North Sea.

Slipper Limpet *Crepidula fornicata* An easily recognised slipper-shaped shell. Length usually 3–5cm. Roughly oval; the resemblance to a slipper is enhanced by an interior ledge extending half the length of the shell. Tends to occur in chains, with the lowest individual attached to a rock or another mollusc, and subsequent individuals on the back of the first; the bottom animals are oldest and female, while those higher up start as males, becoming females later. Originally an accidental introduction from America; now very common, often a pest in oyster beds, around British waters. Empty shells and chains are frequently washed up.

European Cowrie *Trivia monacha* Typical cowrie, similar to the large tropical forms but barely more than 1cm long. Oval, with a slit-like, delicately ribbed opening along one side. Colour variable, from cream to pink-orange or even brown above, usually paler below; usually 3 dark brown spots on upper surface. Occurs from the lower tidal level downwards into shallow water, usually amongst sea-squirts (on which it feeds). Found in the Mediterranean, Atlantic, English Channel and North Sea, though rarely seen commonly. *T. arctica* is smaller still, paler and usually lacking the dark spots.

Pear Cowrie *Cypraea (Erronea) pyrum* A most attractive shell, typically cowrie-shaped, except for being more constricted at one end, giving it an approximate pear shape. It is much larger than the European Cowrie, being about 5cm in length. Both lips of the slit are toothed. The shell is yellowish-brown below, darker and more reddish above, with mottles and stripes. Occurs below low tide mark, usually in rocky areas with abundant seaweeds. A warm-water species, found only in the Mediterranean and Atlantic as far north as Portugal.

Violet Sea Snail *Ianthina exigua* A strikingly coloured, whorled shell, about 1.5–1.7cm long. It has a highly distinctive strong violet colour in life, though the empty shells fade gradually. It is a pelagic species, that floats on the surface using a mucus raft full of trapped air bubbles, feeding on free-floating colonial hydrozoans. Occasionally, shells are washed up, sometimes in large numbers such as in the Scilly Isles after gales. A common species in the Atlantic, though absent elsewhere.

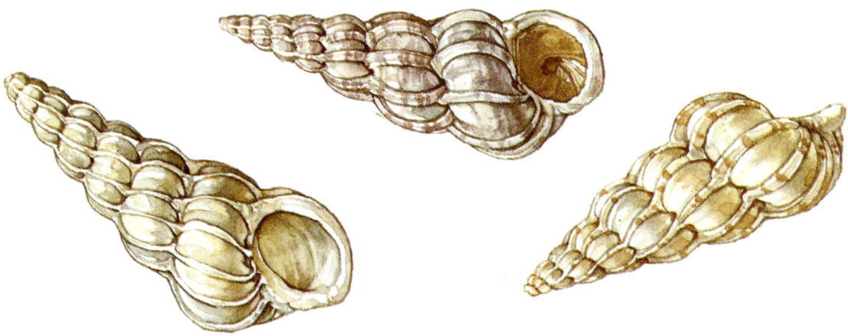

Common Wentletrap *Clathrus (Epitomium) clathrus* Also known as Wendletrap, a beautiful shell, formed of a tall spire with up to 15 whorls, marked with prominent longitudinal ridges. It reaches a length of up to 4cm occasionally more; the strongly marked ridges run along the length of the shell, crossing each suture at right angles. The mouth is circular. Colour varies from pale yellow to reddish-brown. Rarely found living above low tide level, but often washed ashore. Occurs in deeper water, migrating to shallower areas at spawning time. Widespread through the Mediterranean, Atlantic, English Channel, North Sea, and Baltic. Nothing similar.

Large Necklace Shell *Euspira catena* A large snail-like shell, with a strong shine on the surface. It reaches 4–5cm, both in height and width, with 6–7 whorls formed in a very short spire. Colour varies from yellow, through orange, to red, polished-looking and marked with red. A locally common and widespread species that occurs, in life, burrowing in sand from the lower shore downwards, but it is frequently found washed up on sandy beaches. The Common Necklace Shell (*E. alderi*) is common and widespread, similar but smaller with rows of reddish-brown dots on the outside.

Murex *Murex trunculus* A highly distinctive relative of the Dogwhelk. This shell is unlikely to be confused with anything but another *Murex* species, recognisable by its exaggerated sculpturing, peculiar shape and lines of spiny projections. Colour greyish-cream, with brown-blue bands around both the outside and the inside. Occurs in various situations from the lower shore downwards. Found only in the Mediterranean. *M. brandaris* is similar, to 8cm long, but with much more marked long spines, and a very long 'tail' (the siphonal canal) up to 2cm long. Also a Mediterranean species.

Dogwhelk *Nucella lapillus*
A very common snail-like shell, heavily built with a short pointed spire, usually 2–4cm long. Colour highly variable, from yellow-grey to white, sometimes brown and white striped (its colour apparently varies according to diet; the brown-striped version is commonest where mussels are the chief prey). Predatory on barnacles, less often on mussels. Egg capsules are very distinctive, like masses of grains of brown rice, standing on end. Occurs from the middle and lower shore down into shallow water on rocky coasts, often in huge numbers. Found in the Atlantic, English Channel and North Sea.

Sting Winkle or **Oyster Drill**
Ocenebra erinacea Similar in shape to the Dogwhelk, but slightly larger and much more sculptured. The shell is 3–6cm high, with 8–10 whorls and a well-marked spire. It is heavily ridged transversely, with a few ridges running at right angles. Predatory on shellfishes, especially oysters and also barnacles, which it attacks by drilling through the shell. Locally common on rocky and gravelly shores from low water downwards, but coming further inshore to spawn in early summer. Occurs in the Mediterranean, Atlantic, English Channel and North Sea, but mainly western areas around Britain.

Common Whelk *Buccinum undatum* A very familiar, large, robust spiralled shell, frequently found washed up empty. Commonly 8–10cm, though deeper water specimens may reach 15cm; 7–8 whorls, ridged and sutured. The empty shells often provide homes for hermit crabs. The egg capsules are also frequently washed ashore, and the bubbly spongy masses are almost as familiar as the shell. Common on sandy and muddy gravel shores, living on the lower shore downwards, though empty shells may be found anywhere. Occurs in Atlantic, English Channel, North Sea and west Baltic. Spindle Shell (*Neptunia antiqua*) is similar, but smoother; mainly northern.

Netted Dogwhelk *Nassarius (Hinia) reticulatus* An attractively patterned, delicate whelk, with a conical spiral shell. Height usually 2.5–3.5cm. Pale to dark brown, strongly marked with intersecting ridges producing a square pattern. Aperture oval, with a markedly toothed outer lip. Lives by scavenging, unlike most other whelks which are predatory. Common on a variety of shore types, from lower shore into deeper water, though often washed up empty. Occurs throughout Mediterranean, Atlantic, English Channel, North Sea and Baltic. The Thick-lipped Dogwhelk (*N. incrassatus*) is about half the size; found in rocky, less-polluted waters.

Mediterranean Cone Shell *Conus mediterraneus* A smooth shell, almost diamond-shaped in outline, with a long slit-like aperture. It is 4–5cm long, with a compressed spire and a distinctive lower whorl with an aperture reaching about two-thirds the length of the shell. Colour very variable, from yellow to brown, occasionally greenish, and often mottled. Texture smooth and rather shiny. May cause a painful 'bite' if handled when live, from an injection of venom. Predatory. Occurs on sandy and gravelly beaches from low water into shallow water. Mediterranean area only. No similar species.

Canoe Bubble *Scaphander lignarius* An aptly named shell, resembling a blunt canoe or coracle. Usually 5–8cm long, yellowish-brown or creamy outside, sometimes striped; white inside. When alive, occupied by a white or pinkish animal that reaches 14–15cm in length and is unable to withdraw into the shell. Inhabits shallow water areas below the low-water mark, on soft sandy or muddy substrates; normally only the washed-up empty shells are found on the beach. Common in the Mediterranean, and northwards through the Atlantic as far as the English Channel. *Bullaria striata* is much smaller and usually browner; distribution similar.

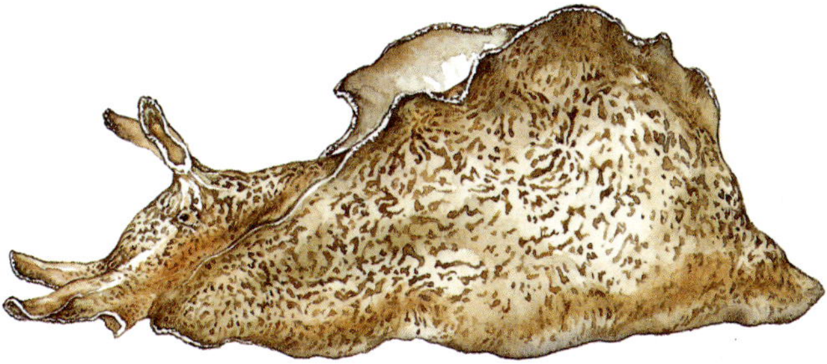

Sea Hare *Aplysia punctata* A strange creature, barely recognisable as having a shell when alive. The animal is large and slug-like, up to 15–20cm, with 4 head tentacles, almost totally enclosing the thin translucent oval shell; varies in colour, according to age and conditions, from red to green. Normally occurs offshore in kelp beds; in summer comes closer inshore to spawn, where it deposits strings of pink or orange eggs. Shell delicate pale brown, may be found washed ashore. Locally common in the Atlantic, English Channel and North Sea. Similar but larger species, such as *A. depilans*, occur in the Mediterranean.

Sea Lemon *Archidoris pseudoargus* Resembles a large yellowish slug. The body is usually 5–7cm long, yellowish with brown, green or pink mottled blotches. There are 2 unbranched head tentacles, and a ring of 9 large much-branched pinkish gills surrounding the anus. There is no shell. It feeds on the Breadcrumb Sponge. Common in shallow water, moving further up the shore from spring onwards to spawn, usually amongst rocks. Occurs in the Atlantic, English Channel and North Sea. There are various related species, mostly smaller; *Jorunna tomentosa* is most similar, but smaller, redder, with 15 gills in a ring.

Common Sea Slug *Aeolidia papillosa* An extraordinary creature, most resembling a marine slug with fur! Reaches 8cm long, but most notable for the dense covering of fine brownish or greenish appendages, which give the impression of fur, usually with a definite 'parting' along the back. There are 2 distinct unbranched head tentacles. Occurs throughout the intertidal area, mainly on rocky shores, especially underneath rocks, where it is easily missed. It feeds on sea anemones. Common in the Atlantic, English Channel and North Sea. *Facelina auriculata* is much smaller, with little tufts of reddish appendages.

Tusk Shell *Dentalium (Antalus) entalis* An aptly named species, most resembling a tiny elephant's tusk. The tapering, white hollow shell is usually slightly curved and 4–5cm in length. In life, a 3-lobed foot projects from the wider end, which burrows into sand, whilst the narrower end emerges into the water. Occurs in sand and mud in deeper water offshore only, but the shells are sufficiently resilient to withstand being washed up. Common in the Atlantic, English Channel and North Sea, more frequent in the north. Similar species, such as *D. vulgare*, occur in the Mediterranean.

Noah's Ark Shell *Arca noae* A large, rather shapeless and untidy bivalve shell. The valves are up to 8cm long, and may be found singly or attached together. The exterior is brown, uneven and often shaggy; interior is silvery. The hinge is long and straight, with numerous small teeth. Occurs firmly attached to rocks or stones by tiny threads (known as byssus) from the lowest shore downwards, though the empty shells may be washed up. Uncommon, found in the Mediterranean and Atlantic only. Similar species include the Cornered Ark Shell (*A. tetragona*), which is smaller and more delicate.

Dog Cockle *Glycymeris glycymeris* Also known as the Comb Shell; large bivalve, with an almost circular shell. The valves may grow to 8cm across, and are pale yellow-brown, marked with rows of reddish-brown zig-zag markings, which look painted on. These markings may be lost in old or well-worn specimens. The interior is white. It is common offshore in muddy, sandy and gravelly water, and the empty shells are often washed up. Distributed through the Mediterranean, Atlantic, English Channel and Baltic. There are several similar species, mainly Mediterranean, such as *G. violascens* which is violet-coloured.

Common Mussel *Mytilus edulis* Occurs in great masses almost everywhere and needs little description, though it is in fact highly variable. Size ranges from very small up to 15cm, and the colour varies from brown to purple and black, though blue-black is most common. The interior is pearly, with a darker border. Occurs abundantly on rocky, stony and even muddy shores, both in estuaries and on exposed coasts, often in very extensive beds. Distributed throughout the Mediterranean, Atlantic, English Channel, North Sea and Baltic. The Mediterranean Mussel (*M. galloprovincialis*) is sometimes thought of as a race of Common Mussel.

Bearded Horse Mussel
Modiolus barbatus Resembles a small, whiskered version of the Horse Mussel, to which it is similar in shape. It reaches up to 5–6cm in length and has rows of whiskers towards the broader end of the shell, forming a shaggy 'fur'. Colour brown-purple outside, paler silvery-blue inside. Occurs on rocky and stony shores from the lowest shore level down into deep water, amongst seaweeds or around boulders. Widely distributed throughout the Mediterranean, Atlantic, English Channel and North Sea, though less common further east and north.

Horse Mussel *Modiolus modiolus* The largest mussel in British waters. Both valves are similar; may reach 20cm but more normally 12–15cm. Shell thick with a horny outer surface, or spiny in young individuals; purple or brown. Interior is silvery-blue and smooth. In life, the animal is dark orange. Common, though not in extensive beds. Occurs from low shore downwards into deep water, especially frequent among holdfasts of kelps. Empty shells are often washed up. Occurs in the Atlantic as far south as northern Spain, the English Channel and North Sea; most common in the north of the area.

Wing Oyster *Pteria hirundo* The exaggerated shape of this species barely resembles other mussels, though it makes identification easy. The two valves are slightly different in shape, both being elongated into a fin-like structure though one is larger than the other. Maximum length is about 7.5cm; the shell is silvery grey-brown outside, pearly white inside. It occurs attached to stones in muddy, gravelly substrates from just below low water down to considerable depths, though shells are washed up occasionally. Common in the Atlantic south from Britain and in the English Channel. Related species occur in the Mediterranean.

Fan Mussel *Pinna (Atrina) fragilis* A distinctive bivalve, resembling a folded fan. This is a large shell, maximum length about 35cm and maximum width about 25cm. The shape is triangular in outline and the colour is usually brown, paler inside. In life, it occurs in sand, gravel and mud, standing vertically with the point buried in the substrate, attached to a stone or other object by fine threads. The empty shells may be washed up. Common in the Atlantic, mainly southern, and the English Channel. Several related species occur in the Mediterranean, including the huge *P. squamosa* which may reach 90cm.

Common Oyster *Ostrea edulis* A well-known shellfish, with ridged circular valves and 'mother-of-pearl' interior. The shell is large, up to about 12cm, variable in shape but usually almost round and saucer-shaped, brown in colour. The exterior of each valve bears a prominent sculpturing which aids recognition. The interior is smooth and pearly-white. Very common in dense beds in estuaries or other muddy, gravelly and stony situations; widely cultivated in commercial beds. The empty shells are washed ashore in large quantities. Occurs in the Mediterranean, Atlantic, English Channel and North Sea.

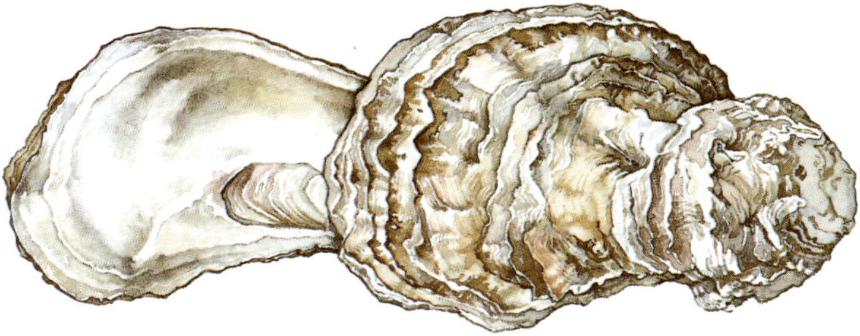

Portuguese Oyster *Crassostrea angulata* Similar to the Common Oyster, though more elongated and less circular; also a rather larger species, up to 18cm wide and 7–8cm long, more irregular in shape. The valves are different, with one being distinctly trough-shaped, the other flatter. The upper surface is pale brown, deeply folded and sculptured; the interior is smooth and white. Imported into British waters from the Bay of Biscay, and now widespread and partially naturalised. Found in similar habitats to the common oyster. Occurs in the Atlantic, English Channel and North Sea.

Great Scallop or **St James's Shell** *Pecten maximus* A large bivalve, with a typical scallop shape. The two valves are different, with the lower valve being rather saucer-shaped, and the upper one flatter. They reach 15cm in length and are reddish-brown with white markings. The 'ears' of the hinge are equal in size. Common in sandy, gravelly and occasionally muddy areas, from shallow water down into very deep water; often washed up. Distributed in the Atlantic, English Channel and North Sea. There is one very similar Mediterranean species, *P. jacobaeus*.

Variegated Scallop *Chlamys varia* A medium-sized, oval scallop. The valves are about 6–8cm across, distinctly tapered towards the hinge, where one 'ear' is several times larger than the other. Colour variable, most commonly purple, red, yellowish or brown, occasionally white, often patchily mottled. The surface is markedly ribbed, and the ribs may have small teeth. When alive, occurs from the lowest shore level down into deep water, either free-living or attached to the substrate by threads. Often washed up empty. Widely distributed and common in the Mediterranean, Atlantic, English Channel and North Sea. Several similar species occur.

Queen Scallop *Chlamys opercularis* A larger species than the Variegated Scallop, with 'ears' more equal in size. The maximum length is 8–9cm. It is very variable in colour, including brown, red and yellow, frequently mottled or striped. The adult is completely free-swimming, moving around in large shoals over sandy or muddy sea-floors by flapping its shells. When young it is attached to a stone or other solid object, but becomes free later. Frequently washed up on beaches. Common and widespread in the Mediterranean, Atlantic, English Channel and North Sea.

Tiger Scallop *Chlamys (Palliolum) tigerina* A small, relatively smooth scallop. Much smaller than the other scallops, with a maximum length of about 3cm. The external surface is usually smooth, though it may be finely ridged. Colour variable, though usually somewhere between brown and white, often with stripes or blotches. The 'ears' are markedly uneven in size. A free-swimming species, apart from in the early stages, though inactive and usually found in crevices or under stones. Empty shells are often washed up. Common offshore, from extreme low water down into deep water, in the Atlantic, English Channel and North Sea.

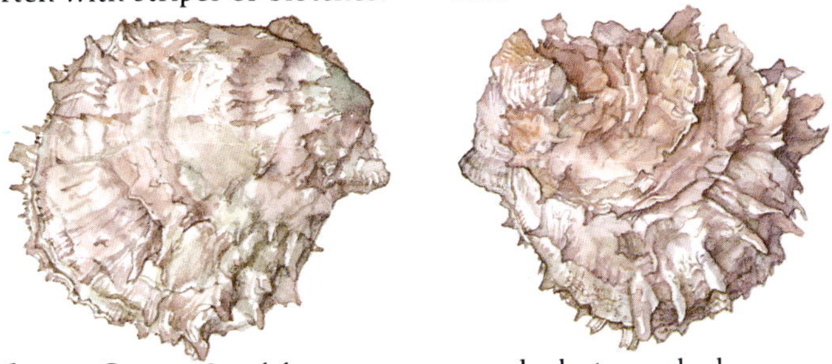

Thorny Oyster *Spondylus gaederopus* An extraordinary-looking shell, armed with numerous thorny projections. It can grow to about 10cm x 12cm. The valves are roughly similar, though one is distinctly more deeply dished than the other, with less sharp spines. Colour is often purple, but may be brown, and often masked by a covering of smaller invertebrates living amongst the spines. The interior colour is pearly white. Occurs offshore attached to rocks or other solid objects. Found in the Mediterranean area only. There are no similar species.

Common Saddle Oyster
Anomia ephippium A large bivalve, up to 6cm long, with distinctly different valves. The lower (right) valve is flatter and thinner, pierced by a hole through which the animal attaches itself to substrates, making the shell appear to be part of the rock. The other valve is larger, thicker and more dished. Both are white to brown outside, silvery-white inside. Common from the middle shore downwards into deep water, attached to rocks or other hard substrates. Widespread through the Mediterranean, Atlantic, English Channel and North Sea. The Ribbed Saddle Oyster (*Monia patelliformis*), is similar but smaller and more ribbed.

Goodalia triangularis A very small cockle-like shell, most commonly white or yellowish. The diameter rarely reaches more than 3-4mm. Both valves have a rounded triangular outline, with strongly marked umbones, and a yellowish-orange periostracum. The shell surface is much smoother than similar *Astarte* species. Occurs offshore in muddy substrates to a considerable depth, in the Atlantic, Mediterranean, English Channel and North Sea. Similar species include smaller individuals of *Astarte sulcata* which is widespread, or *A. fusca* in the Mediterranean.

Spiny Cockle *Acanthocardia aculeata* A large, plump and impressive cockle, also known as Red Nose. Reaches 10–11cm long. The valves are very similar in size and shape, marked by 20 or so ribs running from the umbo to the edge and bearing sharp spines. The spines are distinctly separate from one another. The exterior is yellow-brown; inside pearly-white, with the ridges still visible. Occurs in sandy areas offshore, from about 10m downwards to deep water; empty shells are frequently washed up. Very widespread throughout the Mediterranean, Atlantic, English Channel, North Sea and Baltic. Easily confused with Prickly Cockle (*A. tuberculata*).

Prickly Cockle *Acanthocardia tuberculata* A very similar species to the Spiny Cockle (*A. aculeata*), though generally slightly smaller, up to 8cm. It is distinguishable by the rather more rounded, bulkier shell, the stronger and larger spines, and the rounded tubercles over the lower part of the ribs. Its distribution and habitat are very similar to that of the Spiny Cockle. Found in sandy or muddy places offshore, from about 3m depth; often washed up. Occurs in the Mediterranean, Atlantic, English Channel, North Sea and parts of the Baltic.

Common Cockle *Cerastoderma (Cardium) edule* A well-known and abundant species, whose empty shells are frequently found, valves still joined, on sandy and muddy shores. The shell is about 5cm long; pale yellowish-brown outside marked with concentric brown lines, almost white inside. Numerous ridges radiate out from the hinge, ending in undulations on the margin, repeated inside the shell for a short distance. One of the few properly intertidal cockles, occurring abundantly on lower and middle shores and down into shallow water, often in dense cockle beds. Widespread in the Mediterranean, Atlantic, English Channel and North Sea.

Warty Venus *Venus verrucosa* Large, solid cockle-like bivalve. The valves are up to 6–7cm long, brownish, yellowish or grey outside, white inside. There are strongly marked concentric ridges right across the shell, which break up into teeth or tubercles towards the edge; 3 cardinal teeth on each valve at the hinge. Widely distributed and common in sandy or gravelly areas, from low tide down into deep water. Occurs in the Mediterranean, Atlantic and English Channel. Similar species include the Striped Venus (*V. striatula*), smaller and more finely ridged; and Banded Venus (*V. fasciata*) which is very small (2–3cm) with strongly marked ridges.

Pullet Carpet Shell *Venerupis pullastra* An oval-shaped bivalve with markings resembling the plumage of a hen. The shell is up to 5cm long and about 3cm wide. Valves similarly shaped. It is golden-brown, attractively marked with lines running in two directions. The inside is pearly-white or silvery. Very common from the lower shore down into deep water, sometimes loosely attached by byssus threads, in sandy, gravelly and stony situations. Widespread in the Mediterranean, Atlantic, English Channel and North Sea. The Banded Carpet Shell (*V. rhomboides*) is similar with attractive zig-zag colour banding on the shell.

Rayed Trough Shell *Mactra corallina* A medium to large, but rather thin, noticeably brittle bivalve. Maximum size is about 4–5cm long; both valves similar in shape, like a rounded triangle. Distinct brownish and paler rays run from the umbo to the margin, crossing fine concentric ridges. The interior is pearly-white, sometimes pinky-purple. Occurs in life burrowing in sandy or gravelly substrates, from extreme low water down to deep water, but often washed up empty. Widespread and frequent in the Mediterranean, Atlantic, English Channel and North Sea. *M. glauca* is similar, but greyer, and without the brown rays.

Thick Trough Shell *Spisula solida* Very similar in shape to the Rayed Trough Shell (*Mactra corallina*), though more solid for its size. The valves are 4–5cm long, pale coloured and lacking the brown rays running across the shell. Interior is yellowish-white. Close examination with a lens would reveal that this species has finely ridged cardinal teeth on the hinge, whereas those of the Rayed Trough are smooth. Common in the same habitats and situations as Rayed Trough, with a similar distribution, though this species is absent from the Mediterranean area. Similar species, such as *S. subtruncata*, occur in the Mediterranean.

Common Otter Shell *Lutraria lutraria* A familiar large oval shell, typically covered with a peeling transparent sheath. May reach 13–14cm, though it is more commonly 11–12cm. The exterior is yellowish or brownish and the sheath is often itself brown. The interior is pearly-white. A common species, living buried in sand or sandy mud from the lower shore down into deep water, though very frequently washed up when empty. Widespread throughout the area. There is little else of its shape and size to confuse it with except the Sand Gaper (*Mya arenaria*). *L. magna* is similar, but narrower and smaller overall.

Blunt Tellin *Tellina (Arcopagia) crassa* A solid, rather plump bivalve, with an undistinguished circular-triangular shape. Shell about 6cm long, with one valve slightly flatter than the other, yellowish or pale brown outside. There are numerous concentric ridges around the shell. The interior is yellow-orange in the centre, white on the margin. When living, it occurs buried in muddy sand and gravel, using its two siphons to feed with; frequently washed up, with valves separate or joined. Locally common in the Atlantic, English Channel and North Sea. Several similar species; not particularly easy to distinguish.

Baltic Tellin *Macoma balthica* Similar to the Blunt Tellin, though much smaller and usually more strongly coloured. Shell up to 3cm long; one side of each valve noticeably more pointed than the other. Colour very variable, usually yellow-grey-white, but frequently banded with red, orange, darker grey, or purple. The interior may be very pale through to purple, sometimes banded. Very common in sand and mud just offshore in estuaries, able to tolerate lower salinity (hence its abundance in the Baltic); frequently washed up empty. Occurs in northern parts of the Atlantic, English Channel, North Sea and Baltic.

Large Sunset Shell *Gari depressa* An oval, compressed bivalve, similar to a small Otter Shell in shape. Valves usually 5-6cm long, compressed, both similar, with a definite gap at the back where they meet. Colour variable, usually pale pinky-brown, with darker rays extending from the umbo to the edge; the peeling periostracum is green-brown, the interior pinky-white. Occurs in sandy bottoms from extreme low water down into deep water, though often washed up, usually as single valves. Common in the Mediterranean, Atlantic, English Channel and North Sea. The Faroe Sunset Shell (*G. fervensis*) is smaller and mainly northern.

Peppery Furrow Shell *Scrobicularia plana* A medium to large bivalve, with attractive dark markings. The valves are about 6cm long, each half similar, like a rounded triangle in outline. The external surface is pale greyish-yellow, often marked with a few fine darker concentric lines, though frequently much of the broadest part is dark. The interior is silvery-white. Lives buried in sandy or muddy areas, from the upper beach down into shallow water, and commonly washed up empty; very common in estuaries, and able to tolerate low salinities. Widespread in the Mediterranean, Atlantic, English Channel, North Sea and Baltic.

Pod Razor Shell *Ensis siliqua*
A common and familiar species, the largest of the razor shells, so-called for their resemblance to an old-fashioned razor. The long narrow valves, very similar in shape, with parallel sides, may reach 20cm in length. Colour off-white with brown markings; conspicuous, glossy brown-green periostracum. The external surface is marked with fine vertical and horizontal lines. When living, occurs buried in sand from the extreme lower shore down into deep water, though single or double valves are frequently washed up. Common in the Mediterranean, Atlantic, English Channel and North Sea.

Curved Razor Shell *Ensis ensis*
This species has the familiar razor shell shape, but is much smaller and noticeably curved. The shell valves reach 12–13cm in length, and both margins are curved, roughly parallel with each other. The colour is very similar to that of the Pod Razor (*E. siliqua*). Occurs in sand on the extreme lower shore. Distributed in the Mediterranean, Atlantic, English Channel and North Sea. A third species, *E. arcuata*, is almost as large as the Pod Razor, but is curved on one side and straight on the other; also common and widespread.

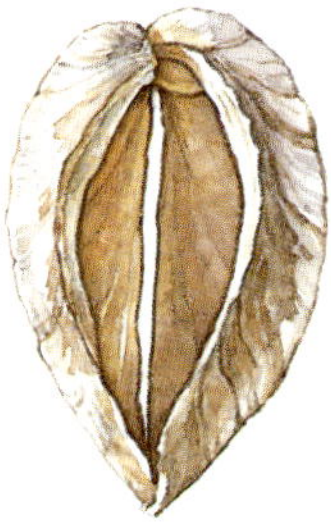

Blunt Gaper *Mya truncata* The gapers are rather like the tellins and otter shells in shape, though this species is distinctive in having one end curved and the other end blunt. The shell may be 8cm long, broadly oval, with a marked gape at one end through which the siphon of the shell projects in life. The external colour is creamy-white to yellow, the inside is pearly-white. It occurs commonly buried in sand and mud from the middle shore down into deep water. Widespread throughout the Atlantic, English Channel and North Sea.

Sand Gaper *Mya arenaria* Very similar in colour and markings to the Blunt Gaper (*M. truncata*), though generally slightly larger and more oval, without the blunt end. Known in the US as the Soft-shelled Clam. The maximum shell length is 14cm. Occurs in similar habitats to the previous species, in sand and mud, though found further up the shore, and is more common generally. Able to tolerate relatively lower salinities, and may be found in estuaries. Widespread throughout the Atlantic, English Channel, North Sea and Baltic.

Common Piddock *Pholas dactylus* The largest of the extraordinary 'boring bivalves'. The delicately ridged, attractive shell may reach 14–15cm long, but is only about one-third as wide. Shape very characteristic, with a distinct projection at one end, and a wide gape. Usually found boring into rock or wood, though also occurs in softer substrates, and may be found washed up when its substrate has eroded. Occurs from the lower shore down into shallow water. Found in the Mediterranean, the Atlantic from south-west Britain southwards, and the English Channel. Similar species include the Flask Shell (*Gastrochaena dubia*), which is much smaller.

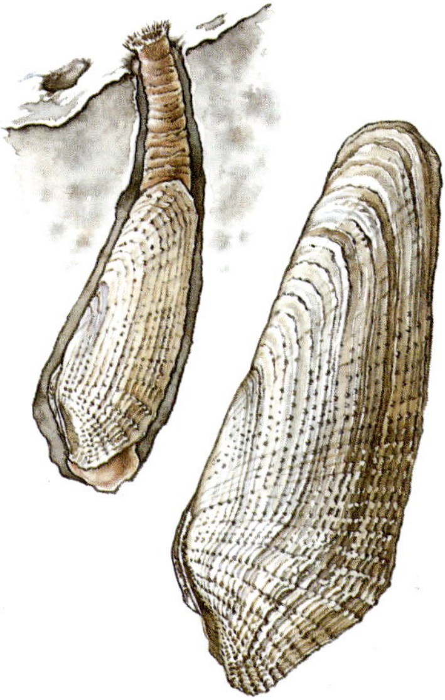

Shipworm *Teredo navalis* One of a distinctive group of shells that live in the wood of ships and harbours. The shell is greatly reduced and functions mainly as a drill, enclosing only part of the animal. The most visible portion is the white, calcareous tube secreted by the animal, which may be up to 12–20cm long. It can be closed off by a pair of hard shutters (pallets) if the animal is not feeding, for protection. Common throughout the area. Similar species include the Large Shipworm (*T. norvegica*), which is often twice as large, and *T. megotara*, usually found in floating timber.

Pandora Shell *Pandora albida* An attractive, rather delicate bivalve, with a crescent-shaped shell. It may reach 3–4cm in length, with a white, finely ridged exterior, often partly covered by the brown periostracum. The interior is pearly-white. The valves are dissimilar with the left valve being concave and trough-like, and the right valve flatter, overlapping the left. Occurs in sandy or muddy substrates, from low tide downwards, living on top of the sand rather than buried in it. Prefers sheltered conditions. Rather local and mainly southern, in the Atlantic, English Channel and North Sea. Nothing quite similar.

Cuttlefish *Sepia officinalis* The 'cuttle bone' of this species is very well known, though the animal itself (a mollusc rather than a fish) is rarely seen. It reaches up to 40cm in length, rather flattened, with 10 tentacles around the mouth, 2 much longer than the rest. The shell is internal, and is seen washed up. Lives close inshore, sometimes found in pools or amongst eelgrass on the lower shore, especially during the summer spawning season. Common in the Mediterranean, Atlantic, English Channel and North Sea; rarer towards the north. Similar species include the smaller and squatter Little Cuttle (*Sepiola atlantica*).

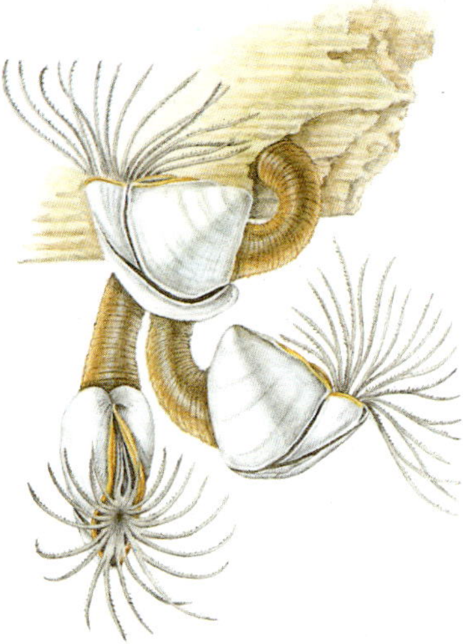

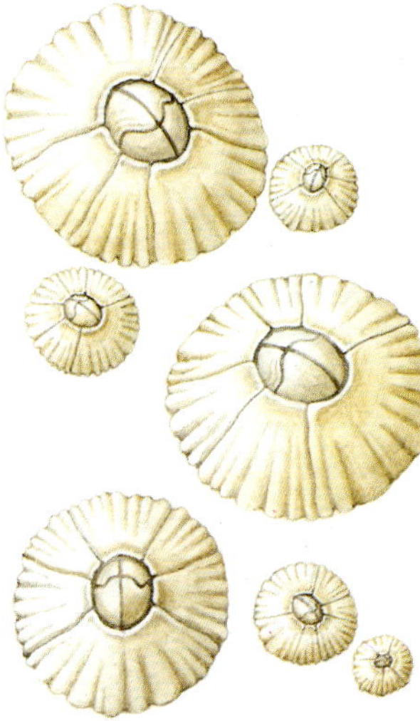

Goose Barnacle *Lepas anatifera* A strange species that attaches itself, by a flexible stalk, to floating wood. The shell is about 5cm long made up of 5 blue-tinged translucent plates, from which the animal projects to feed at one end. This part is attached to floating wood via a long brown stalk that can be partially retracted. It normally leads a pelagic life, floating at sea, but is often found washed up. Widespread in the Atlantic, English Channel and North Sea. The Buoy-making Barnacle (*L. fascicularis*) is similar but smaller and lives attached to its own spongy white float.

Acorn Barnacle *Semibalanus balanoides* One of the very familiar and extremely abundant barnacles that encrust almost every rock on some shores. This species is generally commoner in the north, whilst the almost identical *Chthamalus stellatus* is generally commoner in the south. Where they occur together, *Semibalanus* tends to appear on the lower shore level. The shape and arrangement of the plates making up the shell are different, with *Chthamalus* having 6 more or less equal plates, whilst those of *Semibalanus* are more uneven, and one is distinctly larger than the rest. Widespread and common throughout the area.

Crustaceans

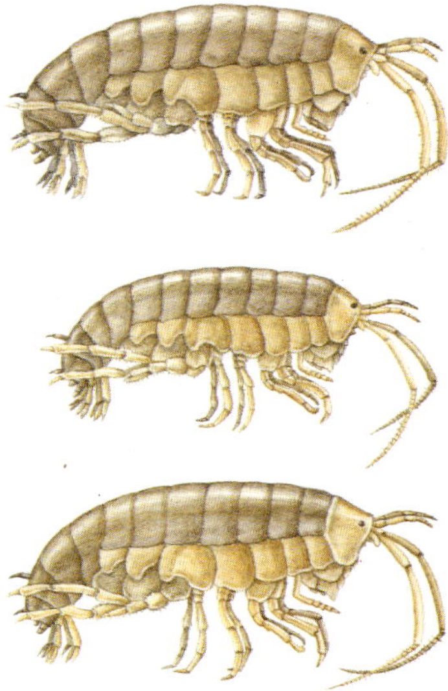

Sea Slater *Ligia oceanica*
Resembles a large woodlouse. The body is about 2–3cm long, with 7 pairs of legs (6 in the female) and 2 large antennae. Very active, especially at night, though fast-moving if disturbed during the day. Grey or slightly greenish-grey in colour, with dots. Lives on the upper shore, especially on rocks and near harbours, hiding under stones or in crevices. Widely distributed and common around the Mediterranean, Atlantic, English Channel and North Sea. The more terrestrial Pill Bug (*Armadillidium vulgare*) is similar, but smaller and able to roll into a ball when disturbed.

Sand Hopper *Talitrus saltator*
One of several jumping shrimp-like animals that live amongst rotting vegetation at the strand line. The slightly curved body is 2–2.5cm long, brownish, grey or greenish, with a black line along the back. Able to jump readily, unlike some related species; masses will spring in all directions if a piece of seaweed is picked up. Very common amongst rotting material, or on sand, on the upper shore. Widespread throughout the whole area, from the Mediterranean to the Baltic. There are a number of similar species, often all classed as 'sand hoppers', which are difficult to distinguish.

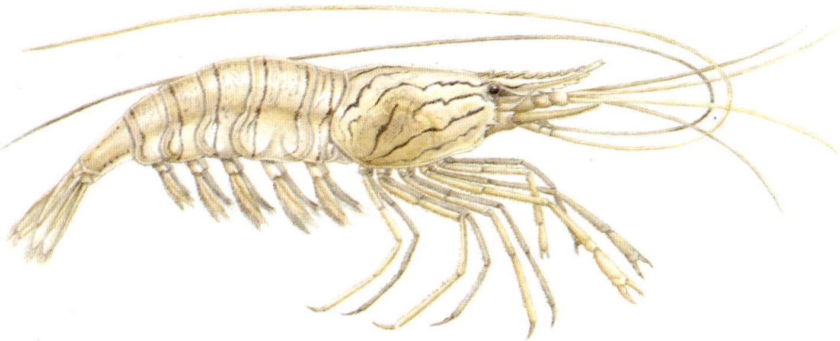

Common Prawn *Leander serratus* The general appearance of prawns is very familiar. Body up to 10cm long, usually 5–7cm; transparent greyish, with coloured dots and lines visible inside. Generally very long antennae, of which at least one is considerably longer than the length of the body. Occurs in rock pools on the lower shore and down into shallow water. Particularly common in seaweedy areas in August and September, varying from year to year. Found in the Mediterranean, Atlantic and English Channel. Many similar species occur, such as *L. squilla* and *L. adspersus*, distinguishable by fine details only.

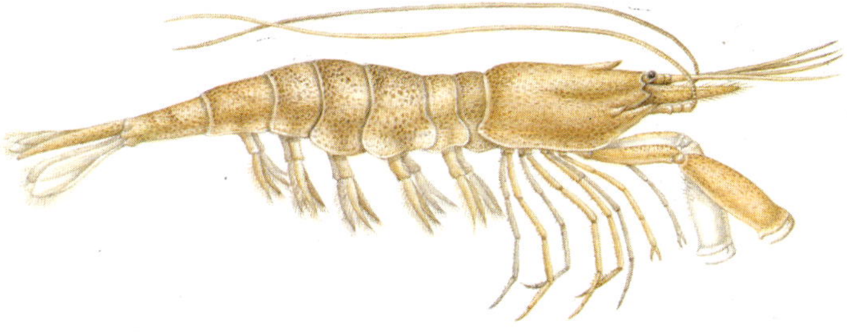

Common Shrimp *Crangon vulgaris* Similar and closely related to the Common Prawn. Generally slightly smaller and slenderer, though may reach 7cm long. Greyish or brownish in colour. The longest antenna is just as long as the body, but not longer as in the Common Prawn. Very common in shallow water, but particularly associated with sandy situations (unlike prawns). May be abundant in estuaries. Widespread throughout the area, from the Baltic and North Sea, south to the Mediterranean. There are several other species of shrimp, mainly smaller, distinguishable only on minor details.

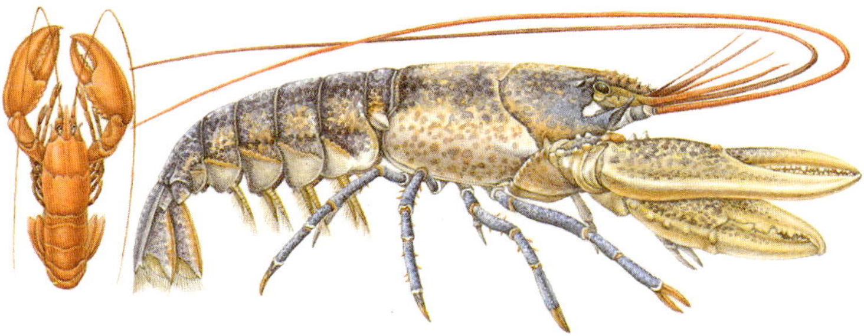

Common Lobster *Homarus gammarus (H. vulgaris)* A very familiar sea animal, though unfortunately usually only seen when dead. Body normally 20–45cm long (though occasionally much bigger); in life basically blue, with small amounts of orange showing through; turns red when cooked. The huge pincers can inflict a painful bite. Widely distributed and locally common in clean-water rocky areas, from lowest tide mark down into deep water, usually under rocks or in cavities. Occurs from the Mediterranean to the Baltic. Similar species include the Crawfish or Spiny Lobster (*Palinurus vulgaris*), which lacks the large claws, and is covered with spines.

Squat Lobster *Galathea strigosa* A strange-looking creature, most closely related to hermit crabs. The squat body, 8–15cm long, is red with variable blue lines. The large pincers, and the main 3 pairs of legs, are all spiny and brown. Occurs locally on the lower shore and down into deeper water, under rocks and stones. Can be very aggressive if threatened. Widespread, but not common, in the Mediterranean, Atlantic, English Channel and North Sea. Similar or related species include *G. squamifera*, which is much smaller and green-grey; and *G. dispersa*, which is small (to 5cm) and dull orange.

Broad-clawed Porcelain Crab
Porcellana platycheles A small roundish crab, slightly longer than broad, which appears to have only 3 pairs of legs (the fourth pair is small, and folded under the tail). About 3cm across in total. Overall colour rather muddy grey-brown, sometime reddish. Large broad pincers are hairy on the outer edges, as are the legs. Widely distributed and common on rocky and stony shores, on the middle and lower shores, often underneath stones. Occurs in the Mediterranean, Atlantic, English Channel and North Sea. The Long-clawed Porcelain Crab (*P. longicornis*) is similar, but not hairy, with narrower claws and a round carapace.

Common Hermit Crab
Eupagurus bernhardus A common seashore animal, well known for its habit of occupying shells; the animal itself is rarely seen fully, since it cannot be pulled out without causing damage. Body varies in size from 3–10cm, occasionally larger; pincers large and coarsely granulated, with the right pincer much larger than the left. Often associated with various other animals such as sulphur sponges, parasitic barnacles, or a sea-anemone (*Calliactis parasitica*). Very common throughout the area, from the lower shore down into deeper water. A similar species, *E. prideauxi*, is slightly smaller, and has finely granulated pincers.

Spider Crab *Macropoda tenuirostris* A creature that appears to be midway between a spider and a crab, though in fact is a true crab. The carapace is roughly triangular, 1–2cm long, dwarfed by the 4 pairs of long thin legs, and the 2 large pincers. Colour is yellowish-orange, though often masked by encrusting growths of algae or sponges. Occurs from the lowest shore level downwards, under stones or amongst seaweeds. Widely distributed and not uncommon in the Atlantic, English Channel, North Sea and Baltic. Similar species include *M. rostrata*, with a less pointed 'snout', and the Mediterranean *M. longirostris*.

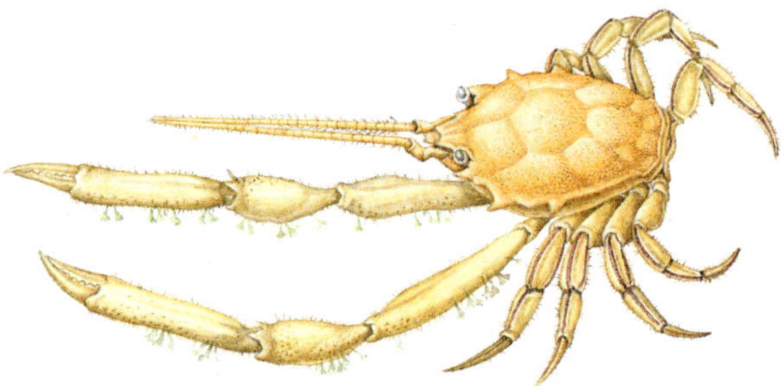

Masked Crab *Corystes cassivelaunus* Notable for its long antennae. The body is about 4cm long, 2–3cm wide; pale brownish-yellow. The pincer claws are much longer than the body; the exceptionally long hairy antennae are joined together for their whole length, and therefore tend to project directly forwards. Widely distributed and not uncommon on the lower parts of sandy shores, and into shallow water, usually buried in the sand, where it can use its antennae to aid the passage of water to the gills. Occurs in the Mediterranean, Atlantic, English Channel and North Sea; rare in the north of the area.

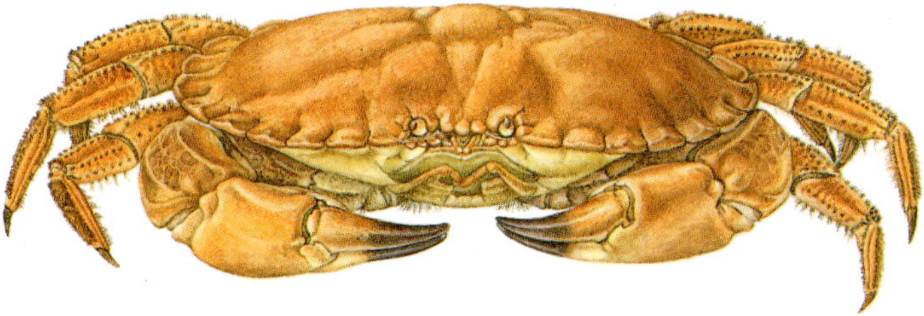

Edible Crab *Cancer pagurus* A large, or very large, crab up to 25cm across the carapace (though usually smaller), with heavy dark-tipped pincers. Overall colour is a rather insipid brick-pink. The edge of the carapace is crimped into a series of lobes, about 10 on each side. The walking legs are hairy, and rounded in section, rather than flattened. Common on the middle and lower shore, especially where there are rocks, and down into deep water. The largest specimens, caught for eating, usually come from well offshore. Widespread throughout the Mediterranean, Atlantic, English Channel and North Sea.

Common Shore Crab *Carcinus maenas* The commonest crab over most of the area. Small to medium sized, 6–8cm across (though much smaller when young). The carapace is brown or green, and has 5 sharp teeth on either side of the eyes. Very common on the middle and lower levels of all kinds of beaches, even in estuaries, and down into shallow water. Widespread throughout the area from the Mediterranean to the Baltic. Similar species include the reddish or greenish *Pirimela denticulata*, which has 7 sharp teeth; or *Xantho incisus*, which has heavy pincers, and a smooth edge to the carapace.

Bristle-tail *Petrobius maritimus*
This insect is a close relative of, and similar in appearance to, the silverfish or firebrat. The silvery-grey body is about 1.25cm long, with very conspicuous antennae that are about as long as the body. The abdomen ends in 3 'tails', of which the central one is the longest. There are 3 pairs of legs, but no wings. Common on the upper shore and above, living in crevices and under rocks, where it scavenges. Can move fast if the need arises. Widespread through the Mediterranean, Atlantic, English Channel and North Sea coasts. *P. brevistylis* is similar.

Springtail *Lipura maritima*
Although individually very small, these little springtails become conspicuous because they live in dense groups. Body about 0.2–0.3cm long, much narrower, dark slaty-blue or grey in colour. Has the typical insect characteristics, if examined closely, of 3 pairs of legs and a pair of antennae. Occurs floating on the surface of rock pools on the upper shore, or occasionally crawling over the rocks. Widely distributed and very common in the Mediterranean, Atlantic, English Channel and North Sea areas. No similar marine species, though there are similar freshwater species.

Sea Spider *Nymphon gracile* An extraordinary creature, with a striking resemblance to a land spider. Body about 1cm long, so slender that it is not adequate to contain the animal's stomach, which extends up the legs. Four main pairs of legs (plus a fifth, much-reduced pair), the longest about 2.5cm. Colour red or pinkish. Reasonably common on middle and lower shores, under stones or seaweed, and into shallow water. Occurs in the Mediterranean, Atlantic, English Channel and North Sea. Other species occur, such as the squat brown *Pycnogonum littorale*, without 'feelers'.

Common Starfish *Asterias rubens* A 5-pointed star-like animal. It varies widely in size, according to age and situation, from just a few centimetres up to 50cm, but is most commonly about 10–15cm across. It has 5 regular arms or points, which turn up at the ends when active; reddish, pink or orange above, paler below. Upper surface is covered by numerous small spines and tubercles. Common and widespread on lower shores, amongst rocks, in shellfish beds, or amongst seaweeds, and down into deep water. Distributed throughout the Atlantic, English Channel, North Sea and west Baltic. Several other species occur.

Spiny Starfish *Marthasterias glacialis* A strange-looking animal, with the typical starfish shape, but covered all over the upper surface with large spines. A large species, up to 75cm across in deeper water, but commonly 20–30cm in diameter; usually greenish, or yellowish to reddish, pale and well-camouflaged. There are 5 arms, which taper gradually towards their ends; these may break off if the animal is picked up. Moderately common, though rarely abundant, on lower shores, particularly where rocky or stony. Often difficult to find. Occurs in the Mediterranean, Atlantic, western part of English Channel and North Sea.

Feather Star *Antedon bifida* A plant-like animal, consisting of a small disc with 5 pairs of long feathery arms. The disc attaches temporarily to stones and rocks, and the arms wave about in the water. The individual arms are 10–15cm long. The animal is usually some shade of red, pink or purple, occasionally yellowish, and the arms may be striped. Widespread but very local, from the extreme lowest shore downwards, amongst rocks and stones. Occurs in the Atlantic, English Channel and northern part of North Sea. There are two rather similar Mediterranean species, *A. mediterranea* and *Leptometra phalangium*.

Common Brittle Star
Ophiothrix fragilis One of a distinctive group of animals consisting of a tiny central disc, with 5 long radiating arms. This species is one of the commonest of the group, which are difficult to distinguish from one another. Disc about 2cm in diameter, pentagonal; arms about 10cm long. Colour very variable, but usually bright red, purple, orange or violet, often strongly patterned or striped on the upper surface. Very fragile. Common on the lower shore, and into deep water, amongst stones, rocks and seaweeds. Widespread throughout the Mediterranean, Atlantic, English Channel and North Sea. Several similar species.

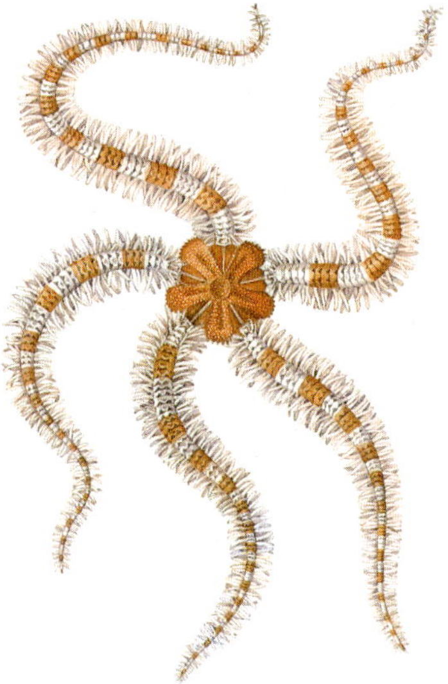

Edible Sea-urchin *Echinus esculentus* A familiar animal, both in its fully spined living form, or as a spineless empty 'test' or shell-like case. The test, an almost spherical ball, is usually about 7–10cm diameter, though it may reach 15cm; slightly flattened at each 'pole'. Spines reddish-pink, often purple tipped, rather blunt. The test itself is red, orange or purple, with the white scars from spines clearly visible. Common, especially in early summer, from extreme lower shore downwards into deep water, amongst rocks, stones and seaweeds. Widespread in the Atlantic, English Channel and North Sea. Several other species.

Rock Goby *Gobius paganellus* One of many similar small rock-pool fishes. The gobies have two pelvic fins joined under the body to form a small sucker on the belly, just behind the head. In this species, the front dorsal (back) fin has an orange band. The general colour is dull brownish or dark grey. Widespread and common in rock pools or among seaweed on the lower shore. Occurs in the Mediterranean, Atlantic and English Channel. There are many other gobies, such as the spotted Leopard Goby (*Thorogobius ephippiatus*), though most are difficult to identify unless examined closely.

Mermaid's Purse *Scyliorhinus canicula* Well known to beachcombers, these capsules are the empty egg-cases of a dogfish. They are laid offshore, attached to seaweed or other substrate by long twisted tendrils; usually the embryonic fish has hatched by the time the case is washed ashore. Each capsule is usually 5-6cm long, (excluding tendrils), brownish in colour, fading later. The egg-capsule of the Greater Spotted Dogfish (*S. stellaris*) is about twice as large. The egg-capsules of skates and rays have points or horns rather than tendrils, though otherwise similar. All are widespread and may be found almost anywhere.

Field Notes

Further Reading

Campbell, A.C., *The Hamlyn Guide to Seashores and Shallow Seas of Britain and Europe*. Hamlyn, London, 1989.

Christensen, J.M., *Penguin Nature Guides: Seashells*. Penguin, London, 1980.

Cleave, A., *Watching Seashore Life*. Severn House, London, 1984.

Phillips, R., *Seashells and Seaweeds*. Elm Tree Books, London, 1987.

Surey-Gent, S. and Morris, G., *Seaweed: A User's Guide*. Whittet Books, London, 1987.

Useful Addresses

Conchological Society of Great Britain and Ireland
c/o Dr Julia Nunn, 24 Park Hill Court, Addiscombe Road, Croydon, Surrey CR1 5PG.

Countryside Council for Wales
Ladywell House, Newtown, Powys SY16 1RD.

English Nature
Northminster House, Peterborough PE1 1UA.

Field Studies Council
Preston Montford Field Centre, Shrewsbury, Salop.

Marine Conservation Society
4 Gloucester Road, Ross-on-Wye, Herefordshire HR9 5BU.

Nature Conservancy Council for Scotland
12 Hope Terrace, Edinburgh EH9 2AS.

Royal Society for Nature Conservation
The Green, Witham Park, Lincoln LN5 7JR.

Scottish Field Studies Council
Kindrogan Field Centre, Enochdu, Blairgowrie, Perth PH10 7PG.

Index

Index